# Bipolar Parent

## Autobiography of Anna Burley

authorHOUSE®

AuthorHouse™ UK Ltd.
500 Avebury Boulevard
Central Milton Keynes, MK9 2BE
www.authorhouse.co.uk
Phone: 08001974150

First published by AuthorHouse 3/4/2011

ISBN: 978-1-4567-7533-9 (sc)

# Table of Contents

# *Acknowledgements*

---

Firstly I would like to thank Briffo. Without your encouragement I would never have been strong enough to put words to paper. To my very dear friend Two Shoes. I would like to thank you for your constant help and advice and just being there for me. You are always a permanent reminder of how lucky I am to have such a brilliant, quirky and mad friend in my life. Thank you for mentoring me and making me laugh about the dramas of the world. I would like to thank my beautiful children for being patient whilst I write and my wonderful husband who hates cooking but was willing to give it a go whilst I typed throughout the night.

# My name is Anna

Its 6.30am on a typical Monday morning. I'm in a deep sleep until I'm awoken abruptly from my slumber by the very loud alarm which is set to radio. This always startles me. On the plus side it brings me straight into alert mode. The news is set at full volume. Only at this volume is it loud enough to wake me. I hear on the news that all of the miners in Chilli have been rescued and smile to myself. I rub my eyes and stumble out of bed. I make the bed in my usual meticulous fashion before jumping into the shower. In around five minutes my children will start to wake and then pandemonium! The usual Monday rush will start. My name is Anna. Just plain old Anna average really. My marital surname is Burley. I fit in like any other adult. I'm very polite and try to ask the correct questions and laugh in all of the right places. My work colleagues and I have a great relationship and I always make an effort with the school mums. From the outside I would be mistaken as a normal well grounded person. My childhood is a lifetime ago and I am a responsible adult now. I tell myself this over and over and sometimes I can nearly make myself believe it. Before I dwell on anything for too long my children burst in the bedroom, arguing who is going to have breakfast first. They push each other to get down stairs as fast as they can. I have no time to think about feeling sorry for myself. There are lunches to be made and children to take to school. Everything is busy, busy. I am rushing around so fast that I do not have time to waste on needless thoughts and insecurities that enter my head. I remind myself of this again and again. Today is starting out the same as any other Monday. As usual, we just manage to get to school on time. But today IS a different day for me. Today is when I decide that I can't run from my past any longer and the memories that I have locked away for so long are itching to escape to the point of unbearable. This is a true story of my childhood. I did not intend to get it published originally. I just needed to rid myself of the person I once was. I have carried around bags of emotional pain for many years in tiny invisible pockets hidden deep under my skin. I lived a childhood of insecurities and needed to eradicate this and to move on. I had buried this little girl deep into the back of my mind. I thought that I could block her out completely. She always seemed to scratch her way back to the surface and because of that alone I could not suppress her any longer. As I started to type and she flooded back into my life. I will continue to tell you my story. But as her, the little girl whose voice can only be expressed in child like emotions. Things may take time to unravel. Please be patient with me I've blocked so much out. It will take time to let go of that pain. There is so much pain that I hold on to.

# Starting from the beginning.

I felt that it was important to give you an insight into my parent's past. Maybe a clue is in there somewhere as to what happens to them eventually who knows? My mother and father were from very different backgrounds. Both of their backgrounds were mentally challenging. My father's family moved to London from Ireland in the late 1940s and were strict Catholics. My mother's family were true Londoners. My mother witnessed mental illness first hand with her own mother who was in and out of different mental institutions throughout her childhood. From a very young age, my mother was pushed out and sent to live with different relatives. She was treated like an outcast for a huge chunk of her childhood. At the age of eight she was taken in by the Red Cross. My mother was a young teenager when she met my father at an exclusive night club, situated in a trendy part of London. My mother was attracted by my father's sports car and his appearance of an affluent lifestyle. My father thought that my mother must be from a wealthy family, as she lived in a prosperous area of London. They were the perfect match. They married quickly. It was the "done thing" in those days. Maybe that decision was made a little too hastily. They both talked about having their own family one day. It was my mother's childhood dream. Money was a strong incentive for my parents when it came to a prospective partner. I'm sure that the physical attraction was also very strong. Characteristics and background meant that they were completely different in so many ways. Many of their family and friends would say their relationship was doomed to fail. They wanted to prove to the world that they could make it. They felt invincible and had their lives mapped out together. They felt their relationship was destined to happen, whatever the outcome. They were blinded by young love. Before the wedding took place, they started to house hunt. Property in the city was too expensive. The chance of finding a home that they could afford in their familiar location was very slim. My father was working in the countryside about an hour away from the city. After a week of travelling there, he drove past a quaint picturesque village. There was a little run down cottage with a "for sale" sign outside just off a main road. The area seemed perfect! Being lead by his impulsiveness, my father took my mother back to view the area and the cottage later that evening. They both fell in love with it and a deposit was placed! My parents married in my mother's local church, pitched at the top of a hill. They were married by her vicar that she had known throughout her troubled childhood. As my father was from a strict Catholic background and my mother's background was Church of England there were tensions from both sides of the families. My Catholic grandmother refused to enter the church whilst the wedding took place. Their photographs showed happy memories. Life for now was good.

A baby was next on the agenda but conception proved to be hard. It took some time for me to come along. Sadly every month the pregnancy test would came back negative. This was strange as she was gaining weight by the day. Her mood swings were erratic and her taste and smell was heightened. However, after the fourth negative test, eureka! I was officially on my way. My mother continued working in the city, until her bump got too big to travel. My parents were now at the next stage of their married lives. Things had shifted up a gear. They were new home owners in a beautiful picturesque village, and they had me. I was the start of their young growing family. Life seemed perfect. At this time it truly was. The cottage needed lots of work. My father decided to smash down and demolish the back end of the cottage. He then covered the entire back half of the cottage with plastic sheeting. Leaving the building completely exposed. That is how it stayed for a long time. We had builders and tradesmen come and go, for what seemed like forever. It became a way of life. My memory bank started to fill with snap shots. I recall one happy memory of a tradesman in particular. He was a family man, a softie at heart. He would plaster the walls holding me with one arm and plastering with the other. This man would soon become a family friend and be part of my comforting childhood memories.

This would be a memory that could bring you back from the darkness. When you were scared and had no comfort. This memory would keep you strong. He was a kind man with a very bristly beard and had a strong smell of cigars. His deep gruff voice always seemed to be soothing. He looked like Father Christmas and had the same round tummy! He would make me chuckle and throw me around like a bag of feathers. I would cry with delight as he swung me around again and again in the gravity free ride. I'm sure that there were many happy memories. Unfortunately family life started to take a turn for the worse. Violence had slowly started to rear its ugly head. There were only subtle changes at first. You may even say unnoticeable. Just subtle mood swings of aggression and short-temperedness. My father was always a very hot headed man with a quick temper. Before long the start of physical abuse on my mother had started. I was toddling at this stage. I quickly learned to always be good. I tried to stay quiet and out of trouble. I didn't make a mess or throw tantrums, just in case. I didn't want to anger him. He was angry so often. This should have set off alarm bells to my mother. She should have got out while she could. She must have loved him so deeply. She didn't get out. She decided to stay. No one took any notice when the violence started in their marriage. It was no one else's business now they were married. Married life was a learning curve and they were still new to love.

# My first memory.

My earliest memory, the most vivid one that I can remember, is a very unusual one. I can remember crawling quite happily in the long grass at the bottom of our garden. I was feeling intrigued by the noises and sights and sounds that surrounded me. The fast flowing water in the river was making an airy whooshing sound. The smell of the river reeds filled my nose with fresh new smell. My sense of adventure seemed to entice me further. My mind was gently urging me to crawl faster. There were new colours, feelings, smells and visions crying out to be explored. All the time I could feel the grass under my skin, the texture was so unusual, changing constantly. It would start by feeling like soft velvet, to occasionally scratching at fragile body. I found myself delighting in the wildlife that was abundant. I could see the ducks and Geese quacking and squabbling and busily taking care of their young. Around me I could hear the loud buzz of a dragon fly and numerous different insects flying busily around me. They were making me jump and squeal with delight. I noticed the clouds whizzing by at such a speed that I let out a loud chuckle that took me by surprise. This made me jump a little. My crawling adventure took me along the River and into the next door neighbours' garden. That was it!

This was the end of my first childhood memory. I don't remember anything else. This is my earliest memory that I can recall. This memory is idyllic. Just like the memory of the kind builder. I sometimes wonder if I made this story up in my head. Maybe it was somewhere to escape to every time the violence began and I had nowhere to run. I could try very hard to put myself there and nothing could hurt me. It could protect me from the years that lay ahead when I could only use the power of my mind to save me.

# My neighbour

I'm sure you are given angels from above. Even if you don't believe in that sort of thing. There are people out there that you meet along the way in life. They are at the place that you can escape to or they are someone that you can learn from. They are usually blissfully unaware of what part they play in your life. Life takes a turn and they become your protector. They may not even realise that they have rescued you. One of our neighbours was an old lady who lived nearly opposite. She suffered from a disorder that rendered her unable to leave her house. Her disability was literally stopping her from breathing the fresh air outside her very front door. I remember her silvery curly hair which still had flecks of black in it and thick black glasses she wore. She whistled when she talked as she had lost a front tooth. Her other teeth crossed over each other. Her teeth were badly stained but I don't recall her smelling of cigarettes. Maybe she was a heavy tea drinker. I found her very curious, maybe mysterious but definitely fascinating. She wore a purple and blue large floral apron which always looked crisp and clean. She always wore thick brown stockings, even in the summer. They always seemed to be wrinkling down to meet her fluffy slippers. I often asked her to come outside, or come over to our house, but mum would quietly bend down to me and tell me to shush. There my mother would stand, on her door step happily chatting away to her for a few minutes. This always seemed like hours to me. This lady was a great seamstress and made all of our curtains for our house. She also played an important part to my earliest memories. I couldn't understand that this lady was standing in her door way but unable to take another step out into her garden. This perplexed me and time and time again I would ask her to come to my house. I can't remember the answer she gave. All I know is she never came. I would pop over to her house on my own sometimes and talk to her on her door step. She would always give me sweets. Her house looked like it was bathed in a continuous veil of darkness. There never seemed to be any light and whilst she would stand in the doorway chatting I could visualise the darkness growing around her keeping her from the outside world. I imagined that there was an invisible force that would pull her back inside and that she could never overcome it. I felt strangely connected to her by the soothing words she spoke and her kind gentle voice. I trusted her. She was another person who I could escape to eventually. The street would also be close to the local nursery that I would attend. Sometimes I hated my mum leaving me there. Then at other times I didn't want her to collect me just yet. I painted pictures. I made new friends, got creative with cardboard and sang nursery rhymes. I remember being very proud of my creative artwork that I could take home. My mind was like a sponge, eagerly learning. I was calculating faces and expressions. I would watch other children's body language and I was beginning to engage on building relationships. I was learning to tackle the world and hopefully win! These were good memories that would set me in good stead for a normal life. A life full of happiness and contentment. These memories were of being wanted and feeling confident with no vulnerabilities and most of all, love. Things change. Life changes, people change and the world whizzes by. They say the moon has connectivity with people's feelings and mood swings. Others say it's genetic, like Bi-Polar. Some people like to blame things on lifestyle. Others blame the drink and drugs. Maybe it's even the situation you're in or the hand that God gives you. Who knows? You believe what you want to believe in, especially when you are the one living it. You tell yourself that this is normal and that this is just life. When it's only your one experience of life how can you compare it to another?

# New home, a better sort of class.

As soon as the Cottage was finished it was sold for a profit and we moved to a new estate. The new place was upmarket, a better sort of class. I started a new school and made new friends. My new friends played outside under the weeping willow tree. I remember having a yellow and blue swing in our garden which had flaky paint. I would peel the paint when I was feeling vulnerable and not sure what to do. When I needed to think. When my parents were arguing and the nastiness had started to rear up again. My ears hurt from the shouting and there was nothing I could do to help. Sometimes I would play out the front with my friends. We had a new designer car which sat on the drive. This would show the road that we looked the part. I think that this was just another materialistic object that would hide the unsettlement that was inside our house. Verbal abuse was a continuous presence in our house now. My mother seemed to have a way of winding my father up. Sadly, it seemed that I would always be the point of the argument. Arguments were constant but at this stage the violence was only on occasions. Sometimes my father would come home late and demand his dinner. My mother would obey. She would make the mistake of asking him for an explanation as to where he had been.

This would turn into yelling abusive words and then occasionally he would feel compelled to hit her. Just the occasional punch started here. Not enough to cause a great concern. Instinctively, I knew I needed to hide out of the way. I would take myself back to good thoughts and block out the surroundings. I concentrated very hard. I had a creative mind and I was able to use it to my advantage and my imagination could take me somewhere safe, for now. My father's moods were erratic. He would flip from being the most pleasant man alive that everyone wanted to know to turning into a complete monster. Strangers would not witness the monster. He was jack the lad who was a friend to everyone. It seemed that whoever met him would love him. Maybe a little too much when it came to the ladies. How could he be so different when he was alone with us? I learnt from a very young age to never answer him back and so far it had worked. He left me alone.

My mother grew fruit and vegetables in the garden and sometimes I would help my mother pick them. There was always the smell of fresh bread being baked, enticing you inside to eat it. The loaf was always eaten before the day was out. My mother loved to cook, she didn't work as such. She helped my father run his business and answer all of his calls. Our house was decorated in a very modern and the top end of trendy in interior fashion at the time. We lived in a small close and close we soon became with all of our neighbours. The people were friendly. They were all of a similar mindset. They were at the same stage in life. Young couples trying to better themselves with 2.4 children. My friend Tom lived opposite with his mum. She was scary. I knocked at Tom's house, it was quiet. He was an only child who lived alone with his mother. On this particular day, Tom invited me inside to play. He offered me a sweet as I walked through the front door from a glass bowl on the sideboard. The sweets looked so pretty, like elegant pieces of glass in different vibrant colours, bright reds, greens and yellows. The glass bowl could have been holding precious jewels and the sweets looked magnificent, very tempting. I took one, my eyes lighting up with pleasure. At this moment Toms mum walked in. I remember looking at his expression and realising that he was scared. He was scared of what he had just done. She scolded us both. I can still recall Tom's scared and shocked face. I remember going home to tell my parents that I had been smacked repeatedly by Toms mum. My mother didn't believe me and decided that that was enough storytelling for one day and sent me to bed. Surely if this were true I would have deserved to be punished. Life seemed a little unfair but hey, I was learning. This was a learning curve about life and self control and to read people and to understand body language. I made a mental note to only invite Tom to my house and to never go to his house again! My 4th birthday was a week away and my parents asked me what sort of present I would like. There was only one thing I wanted. The only thing I had ever wanted, a kitten. She would be small, soft and cuddly. I could love her, look after and cherish her. She would love me back, no questions asked. I would pray for that kitten and keep my fingers crossed the prayer would come true. My birthday was on a Saturday and very early that morning my father took me to the sweet shop in the town. It was one of those old fashion shops that had every kind of sweet in rows and rows of shiny jars, which were measured out by the big scales and put into white paper bags. The shop was bright and buzzing with people. Papers were sold there but what I liked best of all were the rows and rows of boxes of chocolates. These chocolates took precedence in the top row spot and spaced evenly around the entire shop. They were magnificent. They were masterpieces in their own right. They were not any old chocolates but presented in the most beautifully designed and illustrated boxes, tied with ribbons. There were boxes with painted flowers on, china dolls and even pets. Then I saw it. I took a deep breath and gasped. It took centre stage, my eyes widened. Just as the shop keeper wrapped up my little packet of sweets. I gazed up at the chocolate box display. There in all its splendour was a box of chocolates with the picture of a kitten. The kitten I had always wanted and prayed for! My father casually asked me what I was looking at and I pointed at the chocolate box. Oh how I wanted that box just to look at the picture of the kitten. My father shook his head. "Not today, the box was too big and even if I you want a kitten, you need to learn about them first." My heart sank and I sat in silence as we drove home. I remember walking into the house and sent upstairs for sulking. It was quiet upstairs. With the exception of a strange noise coming from my parents room. This was very odd! As I wondered into my parent's bedroom I could hear a curious noise from a box that was under a pile of my mother's clothes. I desperately wanted to open it. The cry sounded needy, and vulnerable. I couldn't stop myself. I moved the clothes and opened the box and there inside was that very same kitten that was on the chocolate box. I couldn't believe it. She was beautiful. She was more than beautiful, she was perfect. I named her Trudy. She had instantly become my number one best friend. At the age of four I only witnessed a few accounts of violence and I knew that many families argue. I only wished that life had stayed like this and not erupted into what was about to unfold. I wanted my life to be full of just kitten memories.

# Childhood pain equals bee sting.

It's strange that childhood memories are innocent until you live an experience. Then slowly your innocence is stripped away. To describe pain can only be done with the experiences you have had or associated situations with. That thought has long since stayed with me. My life started to change dramatically in a very short space of time and my descriptions may seem odd but I still to this day can only describe them as how they felt at the time. Childhood pain equals bee sting. My parents announced that they were having a baby a second child to complete the family. I couldn't wait. There would be a real baby to look after. I started to imagine that I could walk around the street with my favourite dolls pram, pushing the new baby inside. I could teach it all there was to know in the few years I had experienced. The time seemed to pass very quickly and before I knew it mum was as big as a house and the new baby was ready to arrive. I remember driving very carefully to the hospital with my father to collect my mother and our new addition to the family. As mother walked to the car there was this precious little person wrapped up in fine white linen. I had a new baby sister. She smelt of biscuits and felt soft. I felt content and proud and maybe a little bit jealous. She was put in the back of the car in a navy blue carry cot. We went home, now a family of four. We were complete. I did love to talk to her and put her in my pushchair and walk her with my mum around the close. She had a beautiful smile just for me. I was her special big sister. I was very proud of my baby sister. Only I could make her giggle, with the silly things that I could do. I taught her to clap hands and to sit upright. I gave her toys to play with but most of all I gave her lots of hugs and kisses. She was like my own little dolly who I cherished immensely. We were now complete as a family although the atmosphere in our house always seemed a little frosty and unstable. I still didn't know why. I guess with the stresses of family life, there were always going to be ups and downs. Every family has its ups and downs, doesn't it? My mother's birthday arrived and a neighbour came to babysit as my parents went out for a meal to celebrate. Evangeline was six months old and I was now four and three quarters. I can't recall the child minder. I'm sure she was kind and I'm sure she read a story to me and tucked me up in bed. I can't remember anymore of that night. I must have fallen asleep pretty quickly. The next day's events were in contrast to the night before. My childhood pain of emotion bursts out. Everything started to go wrong from here. This was the point of no return. This was the start of the sadness that numbs you. I was the first one awake. It was bright and early. I remember the sun shining through the slits in the curtains. The house was unusually quiet. I wanted to get my usual smile and gurgle from my sister and so I went to her room, I wanted to lift her up and give her a hug and take her into my parent's room, as I did every morning. I remember going to my sister's cot. Her bedroom was at the front of the house and her cot was away from the window.

It was situated on the back wall and you could see her just as you entered the room. I always liked to check on her in the mornings and say hello. But on this day, something felt terribly wrong. I could sense it. The atmosphere was still as I entered her room. Walking into her bedroom I felt cold. The room was deafening with silence. I felt lost, as though I was in a dream, a very bad dream. I looked at her little grey body. She was lying there still and lifeless. She looked empty, she was just a shell. She wasn't moving and there were no smiles or cries. She looked as though someone had made her into a statue. I imagined that she had floated away and even though I could see her body, her soul had disappeared, maybe it would return soon. Even at such a young age, I could see that her tiny lifeless body lay there in the crib, but I knew that she wasn't there. I felt panicky and restless. I didn't know what to do. I called my parents, and the urgency in my voice told them to instantly rush into Evangeline's bedroom. I can't remember who, but I do remember one of my parents crying. This quickly turned into a cry of deep despair. It was a noise I had never heard before. It was a heart wrenching scream and the pain stung me. It seemed to be an endless drone. It pierced my ears and my head and my heart all at once. It felt as though I had been stung by a bee and the pain wouldn't go away. I wasn't sure what was going on. The sting seemed to hurt more and more and I couldn't get rid of it, no one could comfort me. I was in pain and no one could help. My parents couldn't comfort me. They were dealing with their own pain. I wasn't sure what I was to do but I knew that there was panic and bedlam and everything happened at once and then life that stood still for a moment before moving into fast forward. My father asked me to call 999 and before I knew it the ambulance had arrived. The paramedics tried to prise my sister from my mother's arms. I remember her standing in her bedroom doorway shaking with fear. She shook her head from side to side clearly but silently telling them no, no. She was desperately pleading with them over and over again "you're not going to take my baby, you can't take my baby, please don't take my baby away from me" Each time the panic was felt from the paramedics and the sadness, emptiness and distress was etched on my mother's face. I had moved myself into the living room and I was pretending to play. A kind ambulance driver came downstairs to talk to me. He knelt down and told me not to worry he would bring my sister back soon. I waited and waited and waited for her return, but she never did come home. I was never told about her funeral. I know that she had a tiny white coffin and that many people felt the bee sting pain on that day. The day she died is still etched into my head. It's like a scar that sometimes I am able to forget until I accidently scratch it and it brings me back to reality again. I can never forget this particular memory. Although I have wished many times it would leave me, but it never does. It constantly haunts me. Even now after all these years have passed and other thoughts have entered and passed through my head. This one is on a retainer and constantly circulates and arrives back in my head when I least expect it to. Six months later and the mood in our house was still very sombre one. I couldn't quite understand it but something made me feel sad constantly. It wasn't just the death of my sister there seemed to be sadness and resentment dripping out of the walls. Our life was changing and ever so slowly unravelling into ugliness. Arguments had happened before but now there was hatred and despair in our home. As an adult I learnt that my father had began a series of different affairs at this time. My mother knew. She didn't say anything. His affairs had started before they were married. He had stopped for a brief period of time but now they continued throughout the rest of their marriage.

# Broken arm

I read somewhere once that the soul of childhood leaves you quickly without making a fuss. I'm not sure that I ever had a little girl's soul. I had to grow up fast and had to be sensible and have my wits about me. I was different from the other children and because of this loneliness became my best friend. I didn't have any friends at school. At playtimes I would walk around the playground on my own, talking to whatever teacher was there on duty. I would hope that the teacher on duty would be a friendly one. At least I would have someone to talk to. I could just talk about nothing in particular for a little while. The pain and loneliness I had left at home could stay there, at least until it was time to go back home. A group of children decided that I was just weird, a loner and hatched a plan to knock me over whilst I was wandering around in the playground. I was unaware that the children hated me so much and that they wanted to hurt me so badly. I started to talk to a teacher who was on playground duty. Maybe it was my imagination but she also seemed to make any excuse to get away from me. The teacher encouraged me to stop talking to her and go and find something to do. I decided to run around the playground. The children who hated me so much stood huddled in a corner of the playground and waited for their moment. As I ran past them, one pushed me over and the others all jumped on top of me. I fell and broke my arm. The break was so severe that my arm was dislocated and my elbow was in a different place. I can recall going to the headmaster's office and being told that if I didn't stop crying he would break my other arm. He had no patience for me either. I was just a weird kid. I sat in silence. My mother was called and she took me straight to hospital. I was rushed through accident and emergency. I had an x-ray taken of my arm. It was dislocated and broken in multiple places. The hospital made the decision to operate on me straight away. I freaked out, I was dressed in a gown that didn't hide my modesty much and in an operating theatre with lots of strangers, all men. Because my father was so aggressive, I was scared of men in general, they always seemed to hurt or lie to me. There was surgical equipment lined up, shining on the side next to the bed. I needed to be safe, this was going to hurt and I wanted so desperately to be in a safe place, so I ran. I ran around the theatre trying to find the exit, somewhere to escape to. I was cornered and as I fell to the ground, they caught me, crouching behind a trolley. I was given an injection. I don't remember anything after this. I woke up in a bed, feeling sore and on my own again! A buzzer was placed next to my bed to call the nurse if I needed anything. They had placed the buzzer next to the arm that had just been operated on. When I called out to the nurse, she didn't come, so I called her again. Within seconds a deep male voice called out to me to shut up, shut up, shut up, shut up shut the fuck up. I needed the toilet but I was scared stiff that the man would come and hit me. All men scared me now. I cowered under the covers. My bladder felt as though it was going to burst. I daren't move. To my relief, I went home the next day. I went back to school a few weeks after that but I became ill. I had caught mumps. I gave the disease to my parents. I didn't know that my mother was pregnant. She lost her baby. My father became sterile and my parents were unable to conceive once more. "This is your fucking fault" my father shouted at me and I believed him. I stayed cowering in my room. I was desperately hoping that he wouldn't get me. My parent's lives were getting more and more complicated and stresses and strains were constantly with them. I was the cause of the arguments. Everything bad that happened to them was entirely my fault. I was told so continuously, so I started to believe it. I started to just exist on auto pilot. I was too scared to do anything without direct authority. My mind no longer belonged to me and I lost my voice and any opinion that I had. I would even ask to go to the toilet. I was too scared to go without permission. My father now stayed out longer. This was always a relief, but when he returned the arguments would get worse and more aggressive. Very slowly he was becoming increasingly more violent. I found this intensely distressing. These violent attacks always seemed to be unexpected and unprovoked. It upset me deeply to watch my mother being physically abused. Why did he have to hurt her? Why did he have to shout obscenities and make her bleed and bruise her? It seemed that there was a pattern. After any of these out bursts he would rush out and buy her an expensive present and pretend everything was ok. My mother would always come around to his way of thinking. I didn't know the reasons for the arguments or the constant unhappiness they were experiencing. I felt helpless and unable to correct the constant sour taste that lingered in our home. I so desperately wanted to make everything alright. As the anger continued, I always led myself into a false sense of security. I thought the worst was over and this time I truly believed that my father could change. I truly believed that my father could change. But my father's rages just intensified. My mother could not express her emotion. Maybe this was due to her childhood or the years of abuse she had encountered. I too struggled to express any kind of emotion. I learnt to have one feeling only and that was numbness. Numbness was safe and it didn't get me into any trouble.

# Torments

My father's teasing had started now. I remember the threat of an imaginary evil man that would catch me if I didn't run fast enough down the road. Out of the corner of my eye, I could see the thrill on my father's face. He would smirk as he watched me run as fast as I could. I would be physically shaking as I was completely taken over by fear. Trembling and sweating in case I would be killed by the invisible evil man. The evil man could find you anywhere at any time. I truly believed in this man and nightmares about the imaginary evil man would soon start. This man had a gun and a knife. He had evil teeth and could play mind games. I shuddered when my mind accidentally took me to the thought of him. Shortly after the vision of the evil man had been planted, my father took me out for a country drive in the snow. He stopped at a peaceful location. He looked around and made sure that no one was in sight. He said that it would be nice to climb to the top of the hill in the snow to see the view. I reluctantly agreed. I felt uneasy. I instinctively knew that something horrible was going to happen. I was scared, not knowing what would happen next. When my father and I reached the top he looked around and made sure no one was in sight. I'm guessing that there wasn't a single soul for miles.

Then with a smug look on his face, he shouted that the farmer was chasing us and he was angry. He was coming up behind us and he had a shotgun and he would shoot us for trespassing. He would shoot us in the leg first to slow us down and then he would kill us when he had eye contact. I couldn't see him, and I was too scared to look over my shoulder. I started to shake. The farmer was going to really hurt me and I didn't know how to escape. I stopped still. My feet wouldn't move with fear. My father yelled "run fucking faster you stupid child he's going to kill you now. He's gaining on you. Run you stupid shit." I ran so fast, falling and stumbling on the way, snow filling my boots, burning my feet. My little body being involuntary moved in a fashion that was too fast for my frame. I started to feel very sick. The pain that I felt in my throat stung as the wind caught my windpipe. I would sob for ages after this occasion and my father seemed to enjoy this. He looked very pleased with himself. The torments had started. Our neighbourhood now seem a different one too. Our house had become a pit of sadness and the neighbours had picked up on this. They would hide away when we went outside. Curtains would twitch, as we walked past. As I understand it, even though it was a close unit community, people no longer knew what to say to us. On the brief times that we would see someone they would just hang their heads and look away. I don't think that they realised that all we really needed was some laughter. Just a little light heartedness and some kind words or maybe just any words. Just having a conversation would be nice. Funny how people seem to go into freeze mode when there is a tragedy. I look back and hope that it was just out of respect of the death of my sister, but maybe they had learnt about my father's ways. Maybe they knew about the violence he inflicted on my mother and the affairs he had. My mother had another personal blow. Her close friend Carol had discovered she had cancer and after a few months of knowing she died. I knew that she had left our world and that maybe she would be able to look after Evangeline. I would often picture them in heaven, up there somewhere in the clouds together. I would lay on the grass on a sunny day watching the clouds moving quickly and feeling the breeze dancing by. I thought that maybe they were having fun jumping from one cloud to the next, maybe even visiting other members of family and friends, who I imagined to always stand in groups. They would always be dressed very smartly. They would be in their Sunday best. The suits would be black with white crisp shirts and everyone had silvery grey curly hair. Carol left behind two children. They attended their mother's funeral, even though the youngest, a son would only be aged 3. I didn't go to funerals. They were not the place for a small child. Too much had descended on our family and my parents decided to start to look for a new home.

# *A fresh start*

The decision to move was final. The search for a new home had started. Before long a magnificent property came onto the market. It had acres of land and best of all it was within our price range. My parents brought the property with used £50 notes. On the day of completion my parents gathered up all of the notes that were spread around the house. There was money stuffed in jars, under mattresses, in wardrobes and drawers. All of the money was retrieved and stuffed into carrier bags. Then, bundles and bundles of £50 notes were taken to the solicitors. The solicitors would count the money out many times before they all agreed that the money was all there and accounted for. God knows where this amount of cash had come from. No one questioned it. There was something not quite right about this cash. But I didn't know the truth and I still don't to this day!

Our house was bought outright and it stood in its splendour in four acres of ground. There were fields for horses, and an orchard. There was a green house that the previous owners grew fruit and vegetables in. My imagination could run wild with adventures. I imagined that I was wondering through the tropical rain forest trying to make my way out. I felt that I could escape and be happy. We lived in a remote part of a village and I could spend all my spare time walking through the woods that were a stone's throw away. My mind would race and I would be in a fairytale land. When I was in the woods I felt that there was something magical and make-believe. I believed in the faraway tree and fairies. No sadness would get me here. I clung onto that feeling. I often spent my time painting pictures in the nearby fields. I imagined that I was an artist. I sometimes wrote little stories and poems. I was finding new adventures. I spent my time imagining that I owned the woodland and that it was my land. We now had a pet dog. She was wonderful and my protector. She was my best friend. I would call on her in my hour of need and she would always come to my rescue. It seemed that things were looking up and best of all there were no arguments! This truly was a fresh start.

I was always a loner and I still can't remember if I was happy about this or if it just seemed to make sense. How could the other children understand what things had started to unravel in my immature life? Who could comprehend what sadness and uncertainty had affected my home? If they did they probably wouldn't care. I seemed to be very grown up although I now started to long for childish things to do. I started to rebel against my previous childhood years and wanted to fit in. I met a group of local children in the village and joined them on helping out at a neighbouring farm. The farm was owned by a high society prostitute. She would entertain her Arabic friends in the property whilst we mucked out and groomed her horses and frolicked in the hay barn. We spent in the fields with the horses and stables and on top of the haystacks. The local girls taught the boys a thing or two on those haystacks.

This prostitute must have been good at her job. The farm was constantly being modernised and worked on. She must have earned lots of money because new stables and an arena were soon built. There were beautiful thoroughbred horses on this farm. She had started to import and export Arab horses known to be the "purest" of all breeds. She would breed and train these horses and sell them on. The horses in the fields near the front of the yard hadn't been broken. We would dare each other to jump on the back of them. I remember daring a local girl to jump on the back of a horse. She was instantly bucked around the arena and then flung off. She went backwards and somersaulted midair straight on top of the barbed wire. It seemed to take her ages to land. This poor girl looked like she was the main attraction at a circus performance. Suddenly, smack, reality, she landed quite awkwardly. She was winded and out for revenge. It was my turn to mount the horse now, but cowardly I ran away. There was an old caravan on the grounds that spooked all of us! There was a story that a paedophile lived inside. If we needed to pass it we would run past as fast as we could, just in case we were pulled in. We never witnessed anyone enter or leave the caravan. It just sat there rotting away slowly. Soon a local recluse took ownership of it. He wasn't English and his foreign accent was really strong. He was hard to understand. He had a dog called Arse-ole! I remember the man shouting his name up the road in his accent. This would make me feel embarrassed as I would have been scolded for saying such a word. In my mind just hearing the world may have resulted in me getting a punishment. Arse-ole liked to bite. You would have to run like the clappers past the caravan in case Arse-ole caught up with you and bit you. He would snarl and bear his teeth, salvia dripping from his mouth. His eyes were like large dinner plates that would fixate onto you. I learnt to run fast. Sometimes I would play with the man's daughter. If I happened to pass them at dinner time, they would offer me their traditional food. I started to understand the language that they would speak in fluently and constantly but I could never pronounce a single word. I could tell when they were talking about me or my family just by their mannerisms. They would start to whisper and make eye contact between me and the person they were talking to. I would make out that I understood. I didn't like the feeling of someone talking about my personal life in front of me. They stopped talking then. I didn't go there often after that. The local children on the farm would swear constantly. They would taunt me for not joining in. I wasn't cool as I didn't swear. But I was so afraid, afraid that my father would hear me. This was madness as my father was miles away, but I was sure he could hear me wherever I was. I constantly watched what I said, just in case. It was better for the children to pick on me. They didn't know my father! They didn't know what he was capable of. I was more scared of my father than all of the local children put together. Even though he was more than a mile away, he still had control over me. My father had heard me say shit once! I was listening to the radio and there was a particular song playing. Its lyrics sounded like it said the word shit. My cousin was staying and I whispered to my cousin. "I can hear the singer say shit". It made me laugh and my cousin too. As the words left my mouth I could see my father looking at me. I started to panic, he was within earshot! I started to feel sick with worry and what would happen next. "What did you say" he asked, trying his best not to raise his voice in front of my cousin. "Nothing" I said whispering, now panicking, knowing what would come next. "What did you say" he asked again. I had to tell him the truth. He already knew the answer. I was just so scared of the consequences. I repeated back to him, what I had told my cousin. I tried to explain, that I thought that it was the singer that had sung that word, the bad word, the forbidden word. I tried to justify my actions, but it was no use. I was frog marched upstairs and a bar of strong scented soap was cut into cubes and placed on the side of the sink. "Eat it" My father yelled at me. "Eat it you fucking little shit". I reluctantly took each piece and ate it. It took all of my strength not to be sick. He stayed and watched me to make sure I ate each piece, as I gagged he smiled triumphantly as I ate each bit. I was frothing at the mouth and trying desperately not to be sick. He seemed satisfied with himself and told me if I ever swore again I should expect a stronger punishment. Thankfully he didn't physically hurt me. I'm sure my cousin just being there saved my skin that day. This scared me enough, I never swore again. To this day, it is very rare for a curse to fall from my lips!

# New baby
---

My mother discovered that she was pregnant. This was fabulous news for her. I remember seeing my mum overjoyed and telling me that I was the first person that she had told. I felt very privileged. She or my father didn't often share their emotions with me. My soon to be brother's birth was planed out. Even down to the day of his arrival. Before long the day had approached when my father collected my mother from hospital. She walked to the car smiling with a little tiny person in a white shawl close to her chest. He was wrapped up tightly like a little package. There was a new baby but the house was uneasy. My mother rapidly fell into post natal depression. She constantly feared that John would die, just like Evangeline. There were thermometers in each room and the constant methodical checks that had to take place. There were hourly checks of different kinds. First there was the checking of temperature in the room and the temperature of the baby shortly followed by a breathing check, a skin check, a room check, a growing check, and checks of every possible kind. My mother was going out of her mind trying to cope. She was now living in a bubble of constant fear of John dying. She didn't sleep or eat. She just continued with her scrupulous checks. She burnt herself out. She became neurotic. I can't remember if I was just pushed aside or it just felt like it. The little conversation I did have with my parents had vanished and I was only spoken to if I needed to be scolded or to do a task.

I started to resent my brother. This poor baby who had neurotic parents now had a mean sister. I started to become insanely jealous of him. It must have been too much for my parents to take. They were at breaking point. This was not the first hurdle of life struggles for them but this one would push them over the edge. My father started to spend as much time as possible away from home. Not returning until late at night or even the following day. When he was at home he would spend all hours on the phone. My father met up with an old friend who he had not seen since childhood. They would spend lots of time together. This friend owned a yacht and asked my father to join him on a trip. The first that my mother found out was by a note that my father had left in the kitchen. He deserted my mother, me and a newborn baby. He said that he would be off for a few months and would return home when it suited him. He didn't leave any form of contact details or money for food or bills. He just left late one night without saying goodbye. Shortly after his departure I can remember my mother talking on the phone to someone explaining she was not sure when he would return, and if he would return. She sounded worried and scared. Someone was chasing him. Then, before long, more people would come out of the woodwork demanding money or sending threats. My father had been involved with the wrong sort of people and they didn't care who they would hurt. My mother managed to pacify them for a while and sent them on a wild goose chase. I felt constantly sick, never knowing when the next person would knock on the door or if they would hurt us. I now developed a constant tendency to worry. I worried all of the time and felt unsettled and insecure. The little confidence I had seemed to all but diminish. As an adult I now have an emotional scar which makes me worry about everything constantly. I am never able to completely relax and let my guard down. Just in case. After three months my father returned home from "the rebirth of his youth". That was what my mother liked to call it. At the same time lots of strangers would visit our house and shouting and abuse would take place. Now my father had returned it seemed the more time I could spend away from the house the better. I didn't really witness the reality of what was going on inside our house until it was too late. It's funny that things happen gradually and they pass without us noticing. Then when it's too late, things have got way out of control. There is nothing you could do to stop it. Looking back now I realise that there was nothing I could have done. I was a child for God's sake, and whose words were ignored. I was insignificant. But this didn't stop me desperately wanting to fix things and make them right. Being defenceless I did the only thing that could save me and that was to spend as much time as possible away from home. I felt sick that I could never find the courage to fight back. I was a coward and it made me feel wretched inside.

# *Bipolar parent*

I had started to grow up now I was ten years old. I was becoming more independent. My parents were not bothered if I was at home. I wasn't missed if I went out for hours on end. Although I never trusted the local kids and I was quite fickle. I would play with different kids constantly. I didn't really trust anyone. I liked to hang out with the coolest kids from the village. The more rebellious I was the better I felt. I found danger to be a release and gave me a natural high. I felt set free when I was being mindless it was exhilarating. I had to prove my status to the gang. Most of them were smoking now. I began to smoke from thereon too. I thought that I was cool, but more importantly, I was doing something that was rebelling against my family and this made me feel good in a strange and insecure way. Although I found that the feeling of emptiness and loneliness was getting deeper and more uncontrollable. The kids in the gang would also start to dabble in drugs. They started with mild drugs and I would push myself to be the first to try anything new. I soon became totally wild and reckless, craving stupidity. Back at home my mother started to act suspiciously when my father wasn't around. I would catch her on the phone whispering and looking around cautiously. She would scribble things down and hide them quickly. She thought that I didn't see her. I knew she was up to something. I caught her burning bits of paper in the oven. This must have been evidence that she wanted removed. If I questioned her about what she was doing she wouldn't answer me. She just looked panicky and told me to shush. Was I imagining things? She was up to something but I didn't know what. Oh what the hell, it didn't matter. I wasn't wanted nor needed and she certainly didn't want to confess anything to me. Strangely, a few months after my father had returned from his trip he seemed to be calmer and he would even smile at me. It seemed that the trip had recharged his batteries. I was lured into a false sense of security and for a time I really believed that my father was overcoming his anger. Sadly, this was short lived. His temper had always been erratic but now his aggression was at an all time high. He was more violent to my mother than before. He also attacked anyone and anything that crossed his path. He could not be pacified. He would shout obscenities constantly in the house and accuse anyone of anything. He seemed to be suffering from borderline paranoia. He had taken a dislike to our neighbour. Late one night he crept under a hedge and into the man's property. He then stole some railings from his garden. I'm sure it was just to antagonise him. The neighbour had watched in disbelief from his window as my father removed his metal railings from his fence. Rightly so he accused my father of theft. With this accusation my father flew off the handle and told him to "fuck off you jumped up twat." The neighbour came out of his house to talk to my father. Instead of rationalising with him, he head butted the neighbour and then punched him until his nose was broken and his face was red with blood. Then came the look I had seen many times before. My father walked away, leaving triumphant. The neighbour was left cowering in a foetal position waiting for an ambulance to arrive. Now it seemed that his bi-polar had taken over his life and woe betide anyone that crossed him. He was uncontrollable and egotistical. He was like Jekyll and Hyde. It was a Saturday. I was a passenger in my father's car and someone cut across in front of us. My father leaned on the horn and after a display of finger gestures. He told the other motorist to pull over. This was a mistake for the other driver. I was really hoping he would stay in his car. He didn't. I was scared now whispering under my breath, run, run man get back into your car and drive away. In an instant my father punched the man to the ground, hitting and kicking him, the man looked up and pleaded with him to stop. I could see the distress in the man's eyes. My father wouldn't stop or maybe he just couldn't stop himself. The anger was out in full display for passersby to witness. My father could not contain himself. No one would stop to help the man on the floor. I guess they were too afraid. The other motorist was losing consciousness. My father was still going strong. He was seemingly more aggressive with each punch. I continued to watch in horror, trying to hide my face in my hands. This was partly because I was embarrassed but mostly because I was so scared. I really didn't want to watch this. Again I was helpless. I felt sorry for the man. I was unable to defend him. My father would not listen to me and I was too scared to ask him to stop in case he turned on me. All I could do was crouch down under the seat and hide. I pretended that I was somewhere else. I focused hard on one of my many images that took me to a happy place. I knew that what my father was doing was wrong. I knew that you didn't treat another human being like this. What right does he have to hurt someone like that? My father couldn't help it. His anger was his own worst enemy and he was unable to contain it.

I had now realised that my father just didn't know how to deal with a negative situation with words alone. He just didn't seem to have control over his mind. When the anger strikes it just took over. He could only use physical abuse. He suffered with extreme highs and lows. Sometimes he wouldn't even remember doing the nasty things. I'm not sure if he blocked them out or he was just in denial. His extreme anger outbursts were an all too common occurrence. We all feared him in our house. We all did as he said. Next Saturday was sunny so I walked the dog with my father. On our walk we crossed paths with another dog owner. Our dog started to sniff the other dog. The other dog owner tried to pull his dog away and kicked our dog away from his dog. I could see my father's body language change. I knew what was coming. He turned and said "as you have kicked my dog, I am going to fucking kick you now." I watched as this tall well groomed man tried to move away and cowered as my father repeatedly kicked him. Now I was constantly scared of my father. I tried to only ask him necessary things and I tried to stay out of his way. I was so scared of him that if I saw him enter a room I would sometimes hold my breath just so that he didn't know I was there. I was so self-doubting and totally withdrawn spending my childhood feeling numb and emotionless. I was worthless. I was only set free when I was rebellious with the local kids. I started to find that when my father would lift his hand to hit me, my dog would snarl bearing her teeth at my father and let him know that this was not acceptable. She would stand between me and my father, continuing to growl until my father would lower his hand. Funny enough my father would find this amusing and drop his arm down. Thankfully, I would not be hit. My father had an unhealthy interest in dangerous weapons and kept in his bedroom was the biggest machete you had ever seen. It sat in a hand stitched leather case and alongside it hanging on the hook was a shotgun with a belt full of cartridges. I'm not sure if he ever actually used the weapons or if they were just kept for show. My father's movements were too erratic and sometimes he would disappear in the middle of the night. Who knows where he would go or who he would meet? My Brothers first birthday was nearly here. A huge garden party was arranged to celebrate in style. My parents tried their best to mask their unhappiness and acted out the day like a true celebrity couple with the perfect marriage. They hired a magician and a pianist. The day was lovely and the sun shined brightly. All of our family and friends and a few acquaintances would attend the event. The house was buzzing with the noise of a great party and conversations and laughter could be heard across the garden. There was food galore and games to play. The party was a great success. It went on until the early hours of the morning. I could relax at the normality which didn't often seem to be in our house. Amazingly no one ever discussed my father's temper. I wonder how many of the guests really knew my father and what he was capable of. I wonder how many of those men were actually involved in his schemes and if they were equally deceitful. Sometime after the party my mother called me up to her bedroom. She asked me to sit next to her on her bed. There was something sensitive she needed to talk to me about. I was shocked and I felt a little uncomfortable. My mother didn't often hold a conversation with me. As she started to talk, tears rolled down her cheeks and then she started to sob uncontrollably. She was in full floods of tears when she announced that she was filing for a divorce. Finally she had plucked up the courage to leave. She had finally had enough! At long last we would be able to live without constant fear or so I thought. I looked out of the huge bedroom window that overlooked the back of the garden. There I could see my father on his lawnmower as he was cutting the grass. He showed no emotion. The outside world would have thought he was the happiest man alive. The garden was the only thing that seemed to dampen my father's temper. He would concentrate on the job in hand. Maybe it was the fresh air. He put a lot of hard work into the garden which always looked flawless. We had an orchard which in spring the blossom would shower down in petals. I would imagine that it was real confetti and that it was my wedding day. Sometimes I put the petals in glass jars and made my own perfume. This was another one of my many imaginary thoughts that would keep me happy.

We had a bay tree as tall as the house and I loved to crush the leaves and release the scent. There was honeysuckle growing close to the house that gave off a wonderful aroma as you walked past it. This garden would help me too. It was my escape from reality. Most importantly, placed down the side of our house were some very special roses. They were planted to signify the life of my sister. I watched them bloom year after year imagining that the smell of the roses were from Evangeline. If she were alive she would smell of roses. As an adult I always stop and smell roses wherever I am just to hold onto thoughts of Evangeline. There were a few acres at the back of the property that we would rent out for people to stable their horses. It stretched across the back of the land. It was lovely to watch the ponies run around the paddocks. We had two ponies stabled there. They were owned by different people. One pony belonged to a boy with special needs and I liked to talk to him sometimes. My father had built a huge barn where he would spend most of his time when he was at home. He would keep all of his work equipment in there. He also kept his home grown wine in there, leaving it to ferment for years. I can remember treading the grapes and the sensation of the cold squidgy grapes crushing under my feet felt like spiders and slugs squashing through my toes. This was another memory that kept out the constant verbal and physical abuse that went on everyday in our house.

My father didn't accept that the marriage was over. He continued to live in the family home. Amazingly, it was quite amicable at first. My mother would still cook him dinners and do his laundry. They still shared a bed. Life seemed surreal. The divorce was perhaps a little too hasty and maybe they could try to stay together.

The rages had stopped for the time being and family life was ok. It almost felt normal. Maybe a threat of divorce was enough to pull my father out of his bipolar and anger rages. He did seem calmer. Maybe things weren't so bad. Maybe it was all a bad dream and in my head. The next thing was to book a family holiday, somewhere exotic. I thought that this holiday may well fix everything for good. Before long we had packed and we were off to Jamaica for a fortnight. I spend most of my time with a Greek girl who I met there. She was around the same age as me. She became a brilliant friend. We could talk to each with smiles and body language even though we couldn't understand each other. Neither of us knew a single word of each other's native tongue to make any form of verbal conversation. This was a perfect friendship. I didn't have to explain myself or have to justify who I was and what was really going on in my life. Maybe this holiday was just what we all needed. We came back from the holiday feeling refreshed and my mother and father seemed to feel less under pressure.

# Fire

---

As we got closer to home, there was something wrong. The closer we got to our house, the clearer it became. There were high plumes of smoke raging across the top of what looked like our house! My poor grandparents were staying at our house whilst we were away. I started to panic. Were they ok, were they safe? As we pulled up closer, there were fire engines blocking the driveway, the road opposite was surrounded with police cars. I was scared, I feared for my family and my home. What about my grandparents were they safe? What about my pets? Thankfully it wasn't the house itself. Our horse's stables had been burnt to the ground! You could see the fire for miles around. The firefighters tried in vain to keep the flames under control. We were soon informed that the fire was arson. Someone had a vengeance against us. The horses had been set free before the attack had happened and they were not physically hurt. But they were running around like mad in the paddocks in full panic, scared out of their wits, bucking and rearing. It was never clear who had started the fire. The police soon closed the case as there was lack of evidence. My father got it in to his head that a neighbour had started the fire. He said that "the neighbour didn't like the look of the stables, because they were old and needed updating."

My father said that "the neighbour's problem was that he was fucking jealous and he couldn't stand us having so much land." He then raged "He must have fucking known that we were going on holiday. He must have climbed the fence, set the horses free and set the stables alight. The stupid fucking jealous dick. He needs to work harder and get himself a bigger house and stop fantasising about our house". But there was another theory, one that put my father in the frame. The rumour was that he arranged the stables to be burnt down whilst we were away. This was so he could get planning permission to build new stables. Sadly, the permission of new stables was never approved. The application was rejected time after time. There was a coincidence though! The neighbour of whom my father was accusing of arson was also the man he had stolen from. He was the same man who was on the panel of councillors. The reality was that he was never going to approve planning permission. In the end the stables just stayed as a derelict pile of rubble. The fire was too much for my grandmother to take. After she had witnessed the fire, she became ill.

# Physical violence

Things started to get worse at home again and stress and an intense atmosphere was unravelling in to a huge disaster. Now my father was at the highest stress level he could possibly reach. My mother was just about keeping things together. This was always bad and his bipolar and the anger rages were about to rear up again. The talking stopped and violence and yelling began once more. It seemed that just as the physical violence had died down for a while, it started to rear its ugly head once more. It was more intense and this time there was no stopping it. My father just couldn't reason with words anymore. It seemed that my mother would antagonise him with anything that she would do, even just breathing. Things started coming to a head. I was playing in our kitchen with our dog. It was evening and my mother had spent all day preparing some fresh ingredients to make dinner. My mother called me and my father to the table, my father didn't reply. My mother was getting increasingly frustrated. She called my father again. He wouldn't answer her. Now the food was getting cold. We were sitting at the table waiting to start. We were not permitted to start eating before my father. We waited and waited until it was obvious that he was not going to sit at the table. My mother picked up his plate and held it tightly wrapped in a tea towel and walked slowly but in a very matter of fact way out of the kitchen into his study. He was sitting in his high back leather studded chair. He looked like the Lord of the Manor and he was casually talking to someone on the phone. I followed my mother and waited. For some silly reason I thought I could protect her. Instead I stayed cowering behind his study door. I watched her placing his dinner plate on his desk and walking away. Instantly the atmosphere changed. I could feel my body freezing, knowing that something was about to happen. In a split second my father jumped out of his chair and started swearing and yelling continuously at my mother. He was using the most repulsive and horrific words he could think of. After the name calling he stormed out of the study. He was nearly running with his plate into the kitchen. He threw the plate as though it was a discus using his full force. The plate flew right across the kitchen. He didn't care who or what was in the way. It shattered into tiny pieces against the kitchen wall. Fragments of the china plate mixed with gravy, peas and meat flung across the kitchen over my mother, the kitchen, the dog and me. He still continued to shout at her and call her names. There was a chain reaction now. It was as though a switch had been flicked and hatred had set in. The fights would become more physical and severe. I would now hide in the woods. I would sometimes take my tent vowing never to return. I would pack my black brief case and fill it with dog biscuits, pencils and paper and disappear off into the woodland with my dog. I would crouch down in a foetal position hoping that God would rescue me. I would write poetry to keep my mind sane and neutral trying to blank out every memory that I had of my father when he became violent. I couldn't get rid of the images of my father physically or verbally abusing my mother. There were just so many evil outbursts where his violence would make you so scared and you could not escape. My head just seemed to be like a huge camera that would keep all of these snap shots. Those horrific emotional recollections that were increasingly filling in the gaps in my head and I couldn't keep them out. I felt torn apart and uncomfortable trying to grasp the reality of my home life. My mind was constantly investigating why I had to feel so much emotional pain and the physical violence that was constantly at our house. I wanted to know the reasons for this injustice which seemed to be unfolding in my world. Why did I have to feel so neglected and alone again? Was there anyone to talk to? Sometimes I would try to stop him and cry no, no. I would try to stand between them before the violence would become too much. I would cling on to the hope that the desperation and vulnerability in my voice would be strong enough to stop my father hurting my mother but it never worked. I wanted so much to save my mother. It was useless. I was beneath him and I had no self worth. I was the lowest form and nothing I said mattered. I wished that I could escape. I was a part of the dismal violence but with no say and no authority to help or intervene. I couldn't save either parent. I desperately wanted to save my mother from this abuse and my father from the evil demon that seemed to take over his personality. My father's next trick was soon to come a few days later. My mother had decided to follow my father out into his barn. She needed to talk to him. Something uncomfortable was being said and the atmosphere had started to change. I could sense something bad was about to happen. I could hear the familiar sound of shouting outside. But this time something had happened that was different from before. I heard an unusual noise. It sounded like a moan from someone in pain. It made me feel cold. It seems funny in a bizarre way that silence always cuts you like a knife. This silence was deafening. I felt anxious. I climbed up on to the kitchen work top. As I looked out of the window, I could just make out my mother. She seemed to be staggering across the drive. She was acting strange, as if she were drunk. She tried to stagger back from the barn. She didn't seem able to get her footings correctly. She was trying to walk towards me, but she couldn't keep herself upright. Something was terribly wrong. She was now really swaggering across the drive. Very slowly she flopped down and slumped to the floor. Her eyes shut and her body lay still. As I ran out to see what was happening to her I noticed that there seemed to be red liquid everywhere but mostly over her head. The substance was splattered all over her blouse and her speech was slurry but now she had stopped talking altogether. I couldn't wake her, I couldn't move her. In an instant my father appeared. He was in a trance like state and he calmly stepped over my mother. It was as if she wasn't even there. He casually strolled up to our car and popped open the bonnet. He played around with some of the leads. I didn't dare ask him what he was doing, I remember him talking, "There, that should fix it, she won't be able to fucking drive anywhere now stupid bitch" and then slowly walked away. I watched as he strolled back across the gravel drive. I remember the stones crunching under his feet and watching him shut the door of his barn without looking around once. I stood there frozen in panic. I wasn't sure what I was supposed to do. I was too scared to stay at the house. I felt vulnerable.

My mother slowly gained some form of consciousness. I had to think quickly. I managed to half drag her and half stumble with her up to the top of the road. It seemed to take forever. She was heavy and I knew she was still bleeding. I didn't know the extent of her injuries. Finally after what seemed like forever we reached the top of the road and I sat her on an old wooden bench by the side of the main road. It was dusk, but there was enough light to be able to use the phone box. I called the police and they arrived shortly.

The policeman took us to the station and took a statement from my mother. My father had clumped my mother over the head with a brick. He didn't want to listen to my mother. He just wanted to shut her up. He hit her repeatedly until she looked dazed and couldn't speak anymore. He then watched her as she staggered out of his barn. The blood had come from her head. Now the policeman had cleaned her up it didn't look as bad as we had first thought. But she did have severe concussion. After what seemed like hours, we left the police station. We were escorted back by the local policeman. He wanted to check the property was safe for us to enter and take a statement from my father. My father had disappeared. My mother took out an injunction on my father. When we arrived back at the house the policeman looked under the bonnet of the car. I remember the policeman saying "how the hell did you expect to drive away with your head in that state"! This particular policeman became a family friend. He would often change his patrol route so that he would pass our house. He would check up on us making sure that we were all ok. Things were fine momentarily. I think my father scared himself. He didn't realise what he was capable of. I think he thought he had killed my mother. The divorce was swiftly swung into full action. However my mother decided to let my father back to the house and lifted the injunction. This was a mistake as my father's moods were extremely unpredictable. He would take time out and take me and my brother for walks in the woods. When we would be walking deep into the woodland he would cry real tears. He sobbed and said sorry for everything that had happened. I looked into his eyes and he looked so pitiful. I found this hard to accept. I was watching this man who usually carries so much aggression, break down in front of me and cry uncontrollably. I wasn't sure how to deal with my feelings. This would make me choke inside and I would end up crying too. I felt uneasy as my emotions were pulling at my heart. I was not sure of the reality of what was happening. I would try and hold back the tears so that my father wouldn't see me cry. I didn't want him to think I was weak and all of his aggression was acceptable but stopping the tears gave me a sore throat. I tried to gulp down the tears but the cold air would burn my wind pipe. The burning pain was mixed with a heavy aching heart and a head that would spin with confusion. My father would insist that he really did love us. He was confused as my mother didn't want to be with him anymore. He sounded genuine, sincere but how could this make any real sense. He seemed to spend all of his time shouting abuse or hurting her, not protecting her and loving her as I thought a husband should. He still thought she should be with him. He would declare his undying love for my mother. He would bring her home bottles of expensive perfume, jewellery and flowers. Then the following day the arguments and torment would be back into full action. Occasionally I would find them in the same bed together which now seems really odd and quite deranged. I sometimes wonder if my mother had an ulterior motive. Maybe she was doing it to keep him sweet as long as she could. Eventually my mother plucked up the courage to move out of their marital bedroom suite. She set up lodgings in a bedroom further on down the hall.

# *Affair*

---

I came home from school one day to find my dad was at home already. He was upstairs with a stranger. It was a woman. I wasn't sure how to react. It made me feel sick although I didn't know why. I was old enough to know that adults didn't take their friends upstairs. I felt hurt and protective of my mother. I wanted to know what this woman was doing upstairs in my father's bedroom giggling. Then I remembered. I had a sickening thought that I had seen her before briefly before. I was at a sporting event. I remember her face! During the last few years in between the stresses and strains I had been asked by my school to join the local running club. I became confident and speedy. I threw myself into the club. I could now run extremely fast and when I ran I felt invincible. My father would occasionally turn up at different events with a different lady who I would not recognise. The ladies would come and go. My father never came with my mother. I'm not sure if she knew that he never watched me compete by himself. He would wave proudly from the crowd with one of his so called friends, who I would have to meet afterwards. I would pretend not to see him. I would run as fast as I could. I soon became so good that I was picked for the under elevens in my county. This kept me fit and kept me out of the previous trouble I had got into with the local kids. I was able to concentrate on something other than my home life. This particular lady though, made me feel sick to the pit of my stomach. I had seen her before. Now she was in my house, our family home. She was upstairs invading our private space. It didn't feel right. I remember now, during a race night, I can recall looking into the crowd and seeing my father wave. He was smiling. Next to him was a lady. He clearly had his hand on her leg. It was the very same woman!

I ran out of the house and hid behind the bay leaf tree. I tried to gather my emotions and I was trying so hard to be stronger. This was my latest favourite spot to hide when I needed to escape. I was trying to remember a happy place. I tried desperately to find a happy memory from my memory bank. I needed to escape this military run, mental family. My mother wasted no time and put my brother and I back into the car and drove us to see our nanny and grandpa. We stayed at my grandparent's house over night and eventually the following day, we went home. Story after story would come out about my father's continuous affairs. I was told so many stories by so many different people. He was sexually entertaining another woman whilst my mother was giving birth to Evangeline! My mother must have gone through the agonising long pain of labour and all the time thinking to herself what a selfish bastard he really was. How cruel, leaving my mother to go through labour on her own, with his hands in someone else knickers. My mother must have spent every moment thinking about it! The truth was that he was frolicking with some tart. She obviously knew that he was married and due to have a baby at anytime. She would have been stopping him from being there for my mother. My mother so desperately needed him by her side. It wasn't just a one night fling either. It had turned out that he had been seeing this particular lady for some time and enjoyed her company as she was older than him. He could be mothered by her. This wasn't the first of many, many affairs that he had over the years. The affairs had started before he was married and had continued. It seemed that he had a particular type. Usually older ladies and preferably widows! His sex life was as extreme as his mood swings. I was told of his craving for strange fantasies of threesomes and group orgies. There were many women still to come and go. You now had to judge each day as you found it. The atmosphere was very unpredictable with a different mood and emotion for every day. Solicitors and policemen were constantly popping in to our house now. There were also different women my father would bring back with him. The house was very busy and it had become regimented to such an extreme that my parents had court orders on each room. This was ridiculous and the house was no longer a home. Each room had a curfew and rights to each individual parent. All the doors now had huge padlocks that were locked at all times. You could not enter a room without the key. If one parent was occupying a particular room the other parent would stand outside shouting obscenities at the other one. Arguments were the new way of talking. I think normality had left our house ages ago. I had forgotten about Calmness and tranquillity. I tried to stay out as often as possible and started to hang around with the village gang again. I felt isolated. I didn't want to explain what was going on to anyone. I started to become rebellious again. This was the easiest option. I was easily accepted back into the gang as the girl with no fear and would do strange and extreme dare devilish things. The local villagers loved to gossip about my family. It seemed our family was the saga of the year. We were the freak show of the village. I remember one day when I was walking from my house to the top of the road with a group of friends. There were two elderly pensioners just in front of us. We could overhear them talking. They were taking an afternoon stroll along the same strip of road, enjoying the sunshine. I could hear them discussing all manner of sagas that were taking place at a property around the near vicinity. It wasn't until I was close enough to be in true hearing distance that I discovered that they were talking about my house, my family and me. I felt so ashamed. They didn't even know me and certainly didn't know me to look at. How dare they pass judgement on all of my family? I continued to walk behind them. I started to go red and get angry. How dare they feel that they could air all of our personal problems as though it was some kind of soap opera? I felt shattered inside and torn to shreds. I was sure that I was a decent person and no stranger had the right to pass judgement on me and my family. They didn't know all of the facts.

# *Nightmare*

I started to have a reoccurring nightmare. I dreamt that I was running through the woods in the dark. The sky was black and the moon was full. It was cold and the silence was eerie. I could hear the rustling of the leaves beneath my feet. I was bare footed. I would be panting and my throat would be burning. I would try to run as fast as I possibly could. I would run because of the fear. The feeling of the unknown and the sheer anxiety I was feeling. My heart would be pounding and I would feel distressed. A few minutes ago an army of gunmen had invaded my home. They were dressed in camouflage with balaclavas covering their faces. They awoke everybody from their beds. They were yelling at each other to start the shooting. The guns were pointed at point blank range and the firing started. They were killing every member of my family. You could hear the moaning of pain from the shots and the screaming as the realisation had set in that they were about to be shot dead. All I could do was run. I daren't look back. I was making a swift distance between myself and the house. For a split second, I was able to fly. Maybe I could outsmart them. I was back on the ground now. As much as I tried, the leaves were making too much of a crackling noise under my feet. As hard as I tried I couldn't be any quieter.

I changed tactic and I lay still in a nearby ditch. It was vital to lay as quiet as a mouse but my heart was beating so loudly. It was thumping in my throat. Then sudden realisation set in. I knew they were following me. They were there all along. I didn't want to admit to defeat. I was now crawling in a ditch which was nearby to the woodland and it was now early hours of the morning. I was alone and unable to cry in case they heard me. I knew they were out there but I could not see them or hear them. I could just sense them. I had to pick my moment. I took a chance. Now was the time to start moving again. I managed to get up to a neighbour's house, but it was too late. They had been following me all along and had already located my position. They planned their ambush. They found me and came up behind me. I didn't hear them straight away and for a brief moment I thought I had escaped. There was a whisper in my ear. A man was describing to me in detail how he killed each member of my family and left them to die in pain. Then he shot me and walked away. I died alone in the dark laying on the crumpled leaves. My last emotion was fear and sadness and complete emptiness. This dream seemed to be continuous for many years and I still couldn't put my finger on why the dream was so significant. I know there must have been good days. There must have been memories of great days where I was just a child again. I desperately craved those memories where I just had pure fun and I did childlike things. I didn't want to feel insecure and always on edge. I'm sure there must have been many good times but my memory had chosen to blank all of the good times out for now. There were now too many violent memories drowning out the good ones. Most of the day to day violence I managed to blank out. They are still locked away and do not appear in this book. You find that when you live a constant life of violence, you learn to suppress your emotions. I never cried as a child. I learnt from an early age to suppress it. It was a useless emotion that got you nowhere and no one really cared. It just burnt your throat and made you look and feel vulnerable. It showed weakness and people would look at you in disgust if you cried. So it was best to eradicate crying from now on. The next few months passed and the arguments became exhausting. Our local police officer was a friendly face who always seemed to be around when you felt insecure. My father accused him of having an affair with my mother. I was eleven now. My mother started to drink vodka on the nights that my father didn't stay at home and I she would ask me to drink with her. I became her friend, her support and her drinking buddy. My father's bipolar was still uncontrollable and with pure hatred he threw one of her vodka bottles at her head while she was sleeping. He threw the bottle so hard that the glass shattered and fragments were embedded into the wall. This happened one night when I wasn't there. I just remember the chards of glass left embedded in the wall so deeply you couldn't remove them by hand. The fragments were by my mother's pillow. I shuddered to think of how powerless I would have been if I had been there. What could I have done to save her? My mother never really told me how she escaped that night. Or what really happened. I just had second hand information from my grandparents as my mother was too embarrassed to tell me herself.

# Grievous bodily harm.

My father's time spent at the house stopped abruptly. This was because he was arrested. It was a Tuesday morning and we were running late for school. A police car approached our driveway. It wasn't the usual friendly police officer that we knew. There were two police officers walking towards our front door. They knocked and as my mother answered they asked if we knew the whereabouts of my father. My mother pointed inside. My father was in his study, sitting at his desk. He was looking at his paperwork. He seemed calm. The policemen walked into my father's study. He said to my father that they needed a quiet chat down at the station and that they didn't want any fuss. They handcuffed my father and took him off to the local police station. My mother then got us into the car and took us to school. My father was being accused of committing a crime of violence that was so severe, that it was devastating. The accusation against my father was that he had hacked a man into pieces with an axe. This sounded absurd. I had witnessed my father when he was angry, but I just didn't want to believe he could really do something so horrific. My father had gone to help an old friend who was having trouble with his neighbour. An argument had taken place over right of way of a driveway. My father's friend and his neighbour shared a driveway. The neighbour thought he had right of way. The neighbour was making it increasingly difficult for my father's friend to even enter his house due to a car constantly obstructing the drive and property. My father wanted to help out a friend and had just gone to chat to the neighbour. He wanted to make him see reason. He took an axe with him. The neighbour would not listen and my father had lost his temper. The man thought that he could argue with my father. He didn't know about my father's temper. My father went into a calm state of mind and walked to his car. The neighbour thought he had won. He turned around to walk to his front door. He didn't get to enter his house. My father took out the axe from his car. The first strike of the axe hit the man across the legs and the man fell to the ground. The man must have pleaded with him to stop. He must have cried out for help. There were no witnesses. The houses were secluded without any neighbours in ear shot. The man was left in a terrible state. His limbs were severed and he had severe head injuries. My father continued to strike. He was unable to control himself. He repeatedly hacked at the man's body. Finally he stopped. He left leaving the man unconscious. The neighbour spent a long time in intensive care. He was unable to remember anything that had happened to him. Maybe he was just so scared and traumatised to try and remember. I asked my mother why the police arrested my father. She explained that the police thought that he had hurt a man with an axe. They couldn't be really sure at this stage. I decided to become a detective. I wanted to investigate a criminal act of grievous bodily harm. This was just harmless fun. I was only pretending. On my hunt for clues, I noticed that the axe to chop firewood had disappeared. I panicked and ran into the house. I told my mother and wondered where the axe could have gone to? Did she think it was linked to what my father had been arrested over? My mother didn't really answer me and that was the end of the conversation. Before long the day was over and I went to bed. The next day started the same as any other day. My mother collected me from school as usual. She asked if I would mind popping to her friend's house before going home. This particular friend of my mother's was married to a policeman. So on the way home from school that day we took a diversion and stopped at my mother's friend house. Something didn't sit right. I felt very uncomfortable. I was feeling really bad for bringing up about the axe to my mother yesterday. Was this the reason my mother was bringing me here? We all sat around the kitchen table drinking tea. The husband who was a police officer was also there doodling on a piece of paper. I was wondering why he wasn't at work? Conversations were flowing and they asked me about my school life and things in general. I started to relax a little and felt ok to talk. My mother's friend asked about my father and his recent goings on. My mother quite coolly said that I had noticed that the wood axe had gone missing. At this point the police officer had picked up his pen and started to write. Before there was an easy conversation but now there were questions being directed at me and before I could stop myself words were falling from my mouth. A description was being scribbled on the piece paper in front of him. I felt pressured now. At the end of the conversation I was asked to sign the paper that the police man was writing on. I did as I was told to and I signed the statement. I didn't want to hurt my father and I didn't want him to know that this was happening. I felt very ashamed and I didn't want my father to know what I had done. I felt deceived by my mother but I couldn't turn back the clocks. I had just signed a statement of evidence against my father. My mother made her excuses and we left shortly after that. I still felt violated and gut wrenchingly sick. I sat in silence looking out of the car window and wishing that I could curl up and be somewhere else. The guilt was destroying me. My father was kept in custody. There was soon to be a trial date and I was to appear as a key witness. I started to panic. Were they really expecting me to attend court against my father and give evidence? This would prove him to be guilty. I didn't witness anything. The court date was rapidly approaching and this was coinciding with the imminent start of senior school. I felt cross and vulnerable. I was put in a position and I had run out of ways to turn. I felt empty and betrayed. I started to experience panic attacks. My mother decided to confide in an old Doctor of ours and ask for his opinion. They ran a child mental health unit at the surgery and decided to put me under the care of a child psychiatrist there. I remember the lady very well. I hated her. She didn't like me much either. She had brown curly hair and a huge cold sore on the corner of her lip that I used to focus on. Her owl style glasses took over her face and made her eyes look huge and out of focus. I couldn't maintain eye contact with her. The room was a tiny square purpose built office that was two doors down from the Doctors waiting room. There was a pot of dirty colouring pencils, crayons and a few scraps of paper along with some magazines scattered out on a little oak table in the middle of the room. I hated going here so much that I would feel sick before walking inside. My mother insisted that this lady could prove to the court that I was mentally unfit to be a witness. I needed to continue to see this horrible woman. She did write a statement to the court to say that I was mentally unfit. I still had to attend.

# Tablets

I was eleven, could they really say professionally if someone is mentally unfit at this age? I was sure the woman who was psychologically assessing me, hated me as much as I hated her. She never really took an interest in what I had to say. She was never able to look me in the face either. I can remember that she would just ask me to draw about how I felt. She would just read one of her magazines whist I drew pictures. She clearly took no interest in what was happening in my life and she certainly didn't pick up on any of the signs that I was giving out to her. I thought the signs were obvious. I had panic signs that were clearly flashing in bright lights on my forehead. The fact that I had low self esteem and a panic button that was about to blow. It only needed a tiny push and I was nearly there. I started to just answer her when I had to. She decided to tell me that I shouldn't feel sorry for myself as she has other patients with worse problems. She told me about her other patients. She talked about a patient who was under her care. He felt ashamed because he enjoyed having a bowel movement! "There" she said "I should feel lucky that I didn't have this problem." It was after one of these sessions that I went home strong. Strong in the mind that it was time to end my life. I was eleven now and enough was enough,

I was tired of the life I had been living. I wanted to do something about it. I got in the car with my mother for the return journey home. I became really calm and I started to plan. I planned every last detail out in my head and I knew what I had to do. I knew that my mother always brought paracetamol in bulk and that I had read somewhere if you take packets of them you could die in your sleep. I smiled at my mother as we arrived home. I walked to the cupboard where all of the medicines were kept. Whilst my mother wasn't looking I picked out two full boxes of tablets. I poured myself a glass of water and quietly walked up stairs. I had miraculously managed to dull out any emotion I had left. I seemed to be in a trance at this stage and I seemed to have no feelings at all at this point. I sat on my bed and popped out the tablets from the blister packs and touched them with my fingers. I lay them out on my bed and whilst quietly bending forward I rocked and swallowed the first tablet. I began to pick up speed then. I was taking three to four in my mouth at once and drank the water gulping down the tablets. I then sat thinking about everything and trying to reason with myself for being so erratic. After a few moments panic started to set in. I ran down stairs as fast as I could. I told my mother that I had a headache. Ironically she told me to take a paracetomol. I answered in a very sombre tone that I couldn't. "That is impossible. I bought packets of them just a few days ago". "I know" I answered her. Then I had to confess. "Mum, I've taken around forty paracetomol". My mother looked at me in disbelief. She couldn't quite comprehend what I was saying to her. The questions started to flow very quickly now. "How many have you taken?" "When did you take them?" "Why did you take them"? I started to cry uncontrollably.

My mother decided to call my grandfather. He suggested that I drank salt water to make me sick. My mother made a pint of warm salty water. I glugged the whole glass down, but I wasn't sick. My grandfather was still on the phone. He then suggested that I drink pints of milk to neutralise the tablets. I drank so much milk that I had now become quite sick. My mother then decided to put me to bed. She never did take me to the hospital or call a doctor. I don't know why. The next day was a blur and the subject was covered up as though it had never happened. I was still alive and I felt ok. The good news was I didn't need to go to court against my father but the news of his trial did make the local newspaper. Our local newspaper followed the trial from start to finish.

# New school

I had now started Senior School. Before I knew it, news had leaked out that a pupil attending the school was an offspring of the man now nicknamed "the local axe murderer". I knew that soon the whole school would know that it was me. It was just a matter of time. This wasn't fair. I had spent my junior years on my own. I was unable to be friends with other children because I felt isolated. This school was my chance to start over. No one knew me or my past. I had only been here for a few weeks. Now this news would stick with me. I guess I was destined to stay lonely. The rumours grew stronger. There were whispers and guesses what child was connected to this axe murderer. I walked through the corridor with my head down. I was trying not to be noticed. I was on the way to lessons. Someone turned and pointed. She shouted at me "Have you got an axe in your knickers?" Suddenly the corridor that was usually a continuous fast stream of loud people stopped and stared. Eyes open wide and jaws dropped. This girl had worked out the connection. She had taken a wild guess that my surname was connected to the axe murderer. Before I knew it I was known as the girl who carried an axe in her knickers. Now the rumours, the sniggering behind hands and finger pointing had started.

This particular school was a posh school. It was for children to become well groomed. They were expected to achieve exceptionally high standards. I never fitted in socially with the other children. I guess I didn't know how to socialise properly. My exam results showed otherwise. Academically there was promise, but I didn't connect very well with the teachers. There was one particular teacher who I was very fond of. She taught English. Her name was Mrs Greely. She took me under her wing and comforted me. I found her words kind and reassuring. She seemed genuine and her attitude made me feel that there was always a brighter place. Occasionally I would write a few paragraphs about my childhood. I would write about my dog protecting me and how I would feel isolated with what had happened in my life. Mrs Greely would find me at lunch times and discuss what I had written. She read my story as a cry for help and I remember one lunch time she hugged and sobbed with me. She gave me the strength to continue to write about my story and the courage to let my emotions out. At long last the trial of my father's case ended. He was found not guilty due to lack of evidence. No one pointed at me anymore and I started to change and develop. I started to make friends and socialise.

# *Divorce*

Home life was changing rapidly too. Now the divorce was in full swing. Neither parent could agree on terms for anything. Even the decision on who would keep the house was an impossible. Both parents loved the house. They just didn't love each other. They now detested the sight of each other. Finally a decision was made. My father was to buy my mother's share of the property. My father failed to come up with the money. The court gave him time to get his finances together. For now, my mother, brother and I stayed in our family home. It was my mother's decision to rent out all of the bedrooms for an extra income. She placed advertisements in the local papers and lodgers came and went. Our house became very busy. It was constantly full of strangers. There were people with dirty habits and others that just rented the rooms for sex. The house felt seedy and dirty. My house that I once called home became a house with no real feelings and insecurities began to deepen even further. My home had gone from one kind of living hell to another. My life fell apart when one particular lodger came to stay. He asked my mother for permission to let his brother stay for a few weeks. My mother approved it. I was thirteen. I said hello and I was friendly. He seemed like a nice boy. I was young and this boy saw me as vulnerable.

After being polite to each other on a few occasions he asked me if I would go and talk to him in his brother's bedroom. I didn't see a problem with this. He was just being friendly. I was naive. Before long he kissed me. This felt ok at first. He was mature and I felt ok for the moment. Before long he had moved his hand downwards to my trousers. I asked him to stop. I said I wasn't ready for anything like that. He didn't listen. I panicked. I didn't know what to do. I was too scared to scream in case my mother would tell me off for being in his room. I started to feel sick and I felt numb. I took my mind to one of my memories of happiness and clung on to that thought until he had finished. After he had finished, he got up and left. He didn't stay at the house again. My legs had severe bruising along my inner thighs and I bled for days. It felt uncomfortable to walk. Eventually the bleeding stopped. I cried myself to sleep and sobbed my heart out when I was alone. I was just an empty shell with my soul somewhere else. The court hearings about the divorce continued. My father had now decided that he wanted to fight for custardy of me and my brother. On the day of the court hearing he had changed his mind. This was typical of my father. My mother won custody. Before long estate agents were swarming around the house and writing down measurements. They were taking pictures and showing potential buyers around the property. Most of the contents of the house were antiques that my parents had brought over the years. Some pieces of furniture were extremely wacky and very expensive but that was just my parent's taste. The problem was both parents wanted these pieces. Neither would give in. It was a fight to the end. The entire contents of the house had to be auctioned. Both sides of the family attended the auction. It felt as if they were on two teams and I didn't fit in anywhere. There was my father's team and my mother's team! I watched with sadness as each item was bid on and taken away to its new owner. I would look at the winning bidder. Their faces would be beaming. They were feeling very pleased with themselves for winning a bargain. Unknown to them they were taking a little part of me and my life away with them. My life was being sold in front of me. All except one painting. This painting was very special. I could be corrected, but I was sure that this particular oil canvas was a masterpiece by a famous artist. My father had acquired it a few years ago when he had gone out in the middle of the night. This painting now took its pride of place at my grandparent's house. I always enjoyed looking at it. It reminded me of mixed emotions as the years went on. The time was going by at an extremely fast rate now. The house had now been sold to a family who I never met. I had just left my playroom to go down stairs for lunch when something caught my eye. I turned my head to look down the end of the corridor. This was near to where my parent's room was situated. There, at the end of the long corridor hung a picture. The photograph was of me holding my late sister Evangeline. As I turned to look at this picture, I could see a lady who was wearing a greyish white long dress with a veil. She was standing in front of the photograph. She was smiling and holding a baby. When I looked at her again, she just nodded a knowing smile and covered her face with the white veil before disappearing. The feeling she left me was a feeling of happiness and fulfilment. She did not utter a word, but I knew by her actions that my sister was ok and that she was being looked after. I ran downstairs to have my lunch. I briefly dropped into the conversation to my mother that I had seen a lady. I explained that Evangeline was ok and we didn't need to worry about her any longer. I then went back upstairs to my playroom to pack my bags. It was Christmas Eve. I was staying at my father's new pad with my brother for Christmas. My mother told me in later years, that she was so freaked out about my apparition that she packed up her things and drove to her parents and spend the Christmas with them. Things started to slow down again. The divorce was now taking ages to finalise. The house was sold but we were awaiting funds that had been frozen by the courts. Most of the furniture had gone. My mother had no money and ironically we were living in a mansion. We were now living off state benefit! At least the arguing had stopped as my father no longer came to the house. My brother and I got free school lunches. Our clothes were second hand. My mother would go to jumble sales to buy our birthday and Christmas presents. If she had a few pennies left she would try to get clothes for the family. She needed transport and so she bought an old van. It had wooden strips across the roof. They were rotten and the paint was dull and rusty. It would often break down as we couldn't afford to put in fuel or get it fixed. My mother would always carry a bottle of water to top up the leaky radiator. We lived in this strange topsy-turvy world. Now finally, it was coming to an end. At last normality was in sight. I think we were all exhausted and desperately needed to start afresh. With the house and furniture sold, it was time to move. My dog was re-homed. I was heartbroken. She was my best friend. She loved me no matter what. We just couldn't keep her. We had no room for her. For a while my grandparents tried to keep her but she was just too much for them to cope with. I would pray that she lived the rest of her life with a family who really loved her.

# New home.

We moved to a mid terrace council house. What a contrast this house was compared to our last home. The street was full of old cars and there was graffiti sprayed over the walls. Neighbours would stand and argue on their door steps. You could hear trains and traffic all hours of the day. We moved with help from my mother's friend. A man she had met and had a brief affair with. He seemed to be in love with her but my mother didn't feel the same and used him when she needed help. He always seemed eager to oblige and in return he would stay the night. My brother and I shared a room with some bunk beds that were given to us. We had a rusty clothes rail to separate our beds this doubled up as privacy and a wardrobe. We had garden furniture in the living room. We couldn't afford any proper furniture. This house was calm. There were no arguments and no dramatic eruptions. Slowly we started to settle. I had friends from the old village who would occasionally visit. Their parents would now snub us. We were poor and our home was considered a place for down and outs. Their parents would drop them off at the bottom of the road. They would no longer talk to my mother.

My father bought a trendy flat in a local town. He didn't really seem to settle here. I didn't really see him much. Although my mother had custody she wanted us to see him every other weekend. My father tried really hard at first and would take us somewhere special for the day that we spent with him. He loved London and felt happy taking us there. He would always be calm and he seemed to be in control of his temper now. Sometimes we would pop into old pubs where the old London atmosphere could be felt. They would welcome families and we would watch a live band playing. Sometimes we would head down to the docks and see the boats and take in the atmosphere. Other times we would head for china town and have a traditional Chinese meal and Chinese tea and eat with chop sticks. We went shopping in China town. It was very busy. I was looking at the souvenirs. An Asian man grabbed hold of my arm and asked me to go with him. I shrugged him off but he was persistent. He told me that I had to go with him. He kept pulling me, he was relentless. His breath smelt really bad and I started to panic. I saw my father. I struggled free and asked my father if we could go. My father wanted to know why. I was scared and said I would tell him if we could just leave. My father was really calm. Once outside he demanded to know what was going on. I explained to him about the man and that I felt frightened. My father asked me to wait outside with my brother. I knew what was coming. This man didn't know my father. My father caught sight of the man. He called him "fucking scum" and picked him up by the shoulders as if he weighed nothing. He then threw him across the shop. The china smashed everywhere and we left quickly. I was naive. I wanted to find a policeman and get the man arrested. My mother had joined a club for single people. She was attractive and never short of male attention. I lost count of the amount of boyfriends she got through. I had walked in on her having sex with a stranger on more than one occasion. Later on in life she told me that this was done out of necessity to survive. I would still see my father on occasions but he was happier when he was entertaining the ladies or travelling. He turned his back on his family and the problems he had, as though his past life was a dirty secret. He liked living the bachelor lifestyle.

He called me up late one evening and said that he needed to talk. He seemed edgy and hyper. We went for long drive in his car. He didn't want to stop and he didn't want to go anywhere. He was very restless. We drove around and around in circles for an hour. He wanted me to see reason. He went through his life of turmoil and the pain that he had been through. He explained why he had become the person he had and the reason for his marriage breakdown. He came to the conclusion. Everything had failed because of me. It was all my fault and if I hadn't of been there life would have been better. I remember saying goodbye to him. I opened the passenger door and got out. I think that I even leant over and gave him a kiss. I closed the door and waved goodbye. I waited until he was out of site. I then hung my head and ran inside. I couldn't stop the tears and my throat and my nose had begun to stream. My eyes were puffy and red and I was making a snorting noise by now but I couldn't control myself. I cried until I exhausted myself and I fell asleep. I can't believe looking back now that I really started to believe that it was my fault. He really was suffering from a mental illness and his moods were still extreme. I was just a child. I wasn't violent and I wasn't capable of causing a marriage to break up. I believed it was my fault and so began a long spiral of self doubt.

# *Second attempt.*

My second attempt at suicide was no easier than the first and I still feel ashamed by it. Times were getting hard for me, but no harder than before. I had now moved to a new home with my mother and life was calmer. My life experiences had left a dent in my heart that I could not overcome. I became over sensitive and with each knockback I wouldn't know where to turn. I guess because my mother needed to be there for my brother it was easier for me not to burden her with my problems. I came home from school one day to an empty house after a very exhausting and emotional day. I decided that enough was enough. I was going to take the tablets and on this occasion I was not going to tell my mother. I poured myself a glass of water and tipped out the tablets that I had taken from the medicine box. I sat on the third step on the stairs and started to think. I decided to call my friend as a last ditch for help. The poor girl, I can remember the phone call now. She was pleading with me to stop. I tried to explain to her that I could hear her but I could not stop myself. I kept popping in more and more tablets. She was so frightened that she called her mum to the phone. Her mother tried to talk to me on the phone and urged me to think about what I was doing. I could hear the voice but the words had no sense of feelings and

I was tired. Enough was enough. I decided to go along with the conversation. I had said enough to convince them that I was ok. I hung up the phone and took myself to my bedroom. I lit up a cigarette and thought about my life and what I was doing. Life was passing me by and there were so many good times to come. There were adventures to have and people to meet and maybe one day to have a family of my own. I managed to turn myself around. I went to the kitchen and poured myself a glass of salt water. I drank this quickly. I then proceeded to drink the rest of the cartons of milk that were in the fridge. I drank until I was sick. I took myself to my bedroom to think. I then realised from that day onwards that I could spend my time thinking about all of the distress that I had been through. Or I could look forward to new challenges and even though there would be ups and downs. I could now make myself stronger and find the fun in things. I was going to turn myself around.

# New start.

Now things had started to settle at home I was turning into a rebellious teenager. I don't know if this was part of my healing process or just expressing my first taste of freedom. I had a heavy smoking habit and I liked to drink. I now had a best friend who I would play truant from school with. We would spend as much time as we could in London. We depended on each other. We were similar in so many ways. We were both still hurting from our childhood wounds. To keep us sane we would push our rebellious sides to the limits. We would spend all weekend in the city. If we needed to sleep, we would crash out at the all night bars or snooker halls. We were there for each other and we would keep each other safe and out of trouble. We would eventually make it home late on a Sunday. I would walk through the front door to be told that I was grounded but we would do it all again the following weekend. I had started to desperately crave a father figure in my life. A mutual friend introduced me to a local man who was 35. He was Irish and was well respected by the locals in his pub and drove a new BMW. We would spend nights together in his flat learning to play the drums and getting blind drunk and smoking pot. On some occasions we would take walks in the park. I'm not sure why I liked to be with him so much but pretty soon the happiness turned into stone cold reality. The thought of spending time with a man more than twice my age made me feel physically sick. The relationship ended abruptly. Ironically, at this time I was also independent and hard working. Now that I was thirteen, I took on a job at a local shop. This was to support my social life. I progressed from there to a waitress in a restaurant. I enjoyed mingling with the customers and making them feel welcome. I picked up the job very easily. I loved the social aspect and being able to have conversations with people from all walks of life. I was feeling happy and at ease with life. The next two years passed in a blur and I was now fifteen. I spent most of my evenings at work. I still attended school when I could. My life changed again. Something happened to me that would change my life forever. I was about to meet the most important person in my life. This person didn't know it yet but he was about to save me. It was a late Friday evening in mid September. I was just finishing a shift at the restaurant and getting ready to go home. I noticed a group of boys laughing and joking just outside the restaurant. I took a deep breath as I noticed him. This was when I met him for the first time. I was drawn to him straight away. He was talking to another waitress just outside the restaurant. Being flirty I joined in on the conversation. I wasn't in a rush to leave. He had just come back from his holiday. There was something truly special about him. He was kind and shy. I enjoyed talking to him. He looked very well groomed and smelled good! I wasn't sure if he was my type but we chatted and flirted a little. After a while he asked if he could walk me home. I said no. I was waiting for someone. It was the truth. My date didn't show and I started to walk home about 20 paces behind this lad. He was walking the same way with his friends. I enjoyed watching them being silly and laughing and joking around. They didn't notice me walking behind them. I felt safe just being near them. The following week the same group of lads came to the restaurant again and I got my weekly fix of this boy. I felt so reassured when I was with him. He made me feel important and attractive. This became a regular thing and I now walked home with them. They were going my way, what was the harm? The following Friday however, was different. This shy lad who always seemed to pull at my heart strings was pacing outside. He was looking through a shop window opposite the restaurant. He didn't seem to know what to do with himself. My shift hadn't ended just yet but I could help but watch him pacing up and down outside. He looked uncomfortable, maybe slightly agitated. When my shift had finished he asked me if I would like a lift home with him. I asked him where were his friends? Why were we going home alone? I didn't mean to hurt his feelings. He didn't know what to say except "I like you and I wanted to spend time with you". This boy had also had a troubled past. He seemed to need rescuing as much as I did. The drive home was awkward. Although we had spent time together this was the first time alone and this boy was particularly shy. It didn't seem to stop us spending more and more time together. Before long I moved in with him. He was my soul mate and inspiration. He was my positive and a start to a new life. I found him encouraging and he was there whatever the circumstances. We grew up together and argued together. We were inseparable. Before long we decided to move and get a bigger house. We shifted up a gear in our relationship and took it seriously. We went on the most amazing holidays across the Caribbean. We watched the dolphins jump out of the ocean. We got our adrenalin pumping when we tackled the white water rafting. We went whale watching and Jeep driving. We travelled and experienced other countries. We were lapping up the sights and world experiences. We were loving life and very much in love. After our return home we wanted to start a family. After two years of trying, our wish for a family was not to be. Was I following the same pattern of my mother? We endured two years of different type of fertility treatments. This ranged from hostility testing to sperm counting, scanning and ultra sounds. Frustratingly, there were still no signs of a baby. We decided to turn our lives towards a different direction. Now we decided to make a permanent commitment. A rash decision was made to run away to Gretna Green and get married. My lovely boy couldn't keep a secret and told his family of our plan. I had to tell my mother and the trip to Gretna Green was cancelled. Our little wedding dream had now become a huge affair. Before long the joyous day arrived and we had a fantastic day. The week before the wedding, I had my last evasive treatment to help conception. We found that my moods were erratic on honeymoon and I seemed to cry uncontrollably over the two weeks away. When we arrived back from honeymoon I met up with a friend at a local gym and whilst we set about our daily workout she asked me how I was getting on with the clomid tablets. I confessed that I thought they were not working and that I wish my period would hurry up so that I could start the next course. "Do you think that maybe you are overlooking the fact that you may be pregnant". I hadn't thought of that! I jumped up and said that I would go to the chemist immediately and get a test and call her with news either way! The test was positive! I had a little person growing inside me! I was so excited. I couldn't wait to tell my husband. I screamed with excitement as he answered the phone. I was overcome with the amazing news! Before long our beautiful baby was born. The labour was long but it was worth it and my husband had been a constant shoulder to lean on. We took parenting seriously following a routine and putting the baby first, but before long the baby had become ill. To the extent that we had to take her to hospital she would not settle and had a raging temperature and after keeping her in over night the hospital had came to the conclusion that she may have a water infection. They needed to do further tests. Tests that involved invasive treatment and they needed to know if there was any chance that I could be pregnant! I didn't think so but I couldn't be sure and I took a test just to be on the safe side. Oh my God I was! All this time to try to have a baby and two come along at once! After medication, our eldest child made a quick recovery and we took her home with news that there was soon to be another! A few months into this pregnancy, I began to bleed. It was right after I had a row with my mother. My grandmother called to tell me what an awful person I was. It was after this call I started to bleed. I went straight to the local surgery. The Doctor explained that she thought I had lost the baby. She sent me straight to the maternity unit at the local hospital to have an internal scan. The Hospital was brilliant and took me to have the scan done straight away. I was so nervous. I had just got used to the idea of a new baby and now it looked as if I had just lost her. Amazingly, on the screen was a little baby who looked just like a hearing aid moving around quite happily. I was soon discharged and told that the baby was fine. I was so relieved that I cried for an hour. This baby was different from the last. She was erratic and constantly moved around to the point of exhaustion! The hospital monitored me closely. They were worried about her heart as she was constantly switched to high-speed. The baby arrived quickly and the labour was in vast contrast to the last. The baby was a happy but busy little girl who was in a desperate need to do things! She needed to walk, talk, eat and drink before any other child her age. When she could achieve her first milestones she would be trying to accomplish the next lot of milestones. She never stopped. She was (and still is) exhausting! Her behaviour is erratic and as soon as she could verbalise her emotions her anger would appear from nowhere. She would get easily frustrated and she had a strong temper on her. I now started to wonder about mental health and genetics! Did my child have bipolar? Is bipolar affecting my father? Is it now affecting my daughter? Was bi-polar hereditary? I had lots of questions flowing through my mind. I couldn't seem to find the answers. I couldn't seem to get any help from anyone. Even the professionals would fob us off with half of the answer and yet another person to contact. I took my daughter to the local doctor first. She said she could not help and that she would contact the local council and get her referred. The local council could not deal with us so they passed us on to the school nurse! The only problem was the school that my daughter attended didn't have a school nurse. I was at the end of the line. Was I hitting my head against a brick wall? There seemed to be no help anywhere and I desperately needed to help my daughter. I just had to face it. I was stuck for the time being and just had to wait and see what would unveil. I tried not to worry and I reminded myself that we did have a good life. It was full of materialistic things and money came easy to us. But this wasn't enough and we didn't seem to be living life to its full potential. We craved change and quality family time. I wanted to offer my children the best that I could. It was now time to make something of ourselves and try to offer our children a better quality of life and if possible in a better climate. We craved a lifestyle with a relaxed culture. Maybe this would help calm down my daughters mood swings and erratic behaviour. We decided to try a life changing experience. We started to look at migrating to another country. Maybe we were running away from reality who knows. We took our dream and turned it into a reality and before long we migrated to Australia. Our first stop was Melbourne where we were warmly greeted by long distant family. They had kindly set us up with a house. It was a traditional weather boarded property. It included a garden full of fruit and vegetables so that we could become self sufficient. We would gaze in wonder at the wildlife. We took a deep breath in and enjoyed the natural world around us. We lived near a natural wetland and would cycle around lakes and the ocean with the girls. It took no time to settle and the children had soon started the local school. We met some lovely friends and started to become involved with the local area. The children could be themselves. The locals were used to loud kids. They made no secret that all Aussie kids were feral! We spent our time on the local beaches and across quaint little towns. We enjoyed sights that we had never seen before. The girls loved the nature and enjoyed the natural life as much as we did. Melbourne was a very cosmopolitan city. It reminded us of England in so many ways that we craved for a change again and before long it was time for us to move on. We took a plane to Perth and we were blown away by the kindness of the local people and the cleanliness of the place. We decided to stop here for a while. The Anzac procession was taking place. We watched as the locals paid their respects. We admired the values that the people here held. The people here really seemed to care about each other. We enjoyed the local sights and the natural beauty of the place. We took a tree top walk across Perth's national park and admired the city. It was relaxing to feel the breeze in our hair and sand in our toes as we walked along the ocean front. We found a property here that we really liked. We made a spontaneous decision to buy it and put in an offer with our fingers crossed. We hoped that the offer would be accepted. We could then fly back to Melbourne and collect our stuff and return straight back to Perth. Unfortunately the offer was declined. The decision was made for us. We bought a property in an up and coming part of Melbourne. A few months after moving into the house I sank into depression. It was the loneliness. My husband was working shifts and we didn't see each other. We were living in a new area with no neighbours close by. Whilst the children were at school I would take myself to the local natural beach. It was always very windy and I would sit there staring across the ocean until my body became numb from the cold. Then I would slowly drive back home again. Bad emotions had started to take over and I was feeling very low. The dulling down of any happy feelings had started to break me down. Old emotions that had affected me as a child seemed to be coming back to me. My husband was working nights and I was working days and the isolation was eating me up inside. It was at that point that I had received a call from my mother letting us know that she wanted to visit us in Australia. She didn't like Melbourne so she would pay for us to fly up to Cairns and meet us there! My mind started to go into overdrive! I started to hatch a plan. What if we could rent out the house in Melbourne and move to Brisbane. It sounded brilliant! All I needed to do was to convince my husband! He could see how depressed and withdrawn I had become. He worried about me and reluctantly agreed to make the move across to Brisbane. We started to make plans and we rented out the house in no time. We took an internal flight and our beloved jeep with us too! It was lovely to see my mother but also very emotional. We cried for ages with our bodies shuddering uncontrollably with emotion. It had seemed that she had just been a distant memory for a long time and then suddenly she was there in front of me. It was quite surreal. I have always had a strange relationship with my mother. We have never really understood each other. We can be so close but so far apart. We are still strangely attached. My mother can be with you physically but mentally she would be somewhere else. She would answer you if you spoke to her but she never really listened to any words that you had to say. It would always be frustrating as she would not remember dates or important things that you had told her. Putting all of the past behind us we had a really lovely holiday and really enjoyed each other's company. We went to the local theme parks and made our way to Surfers Paradise. We took a boat and went snorkelling. I can still remember the squeals of delight from the children when they could see the fish. This was such an amazing experience one that you would remember for a lifetime. It was soon time to say goodbye to my mother. Our life journey was about to start again. We didn't have a house or a job or an area to go to. As we started to drive towards Brisbane It soon became clear it wasn't what we had expected. It seemed to be much like Melbourne. Brisbane was another huge city and although it was clean, it wasn't the small town area steeped in natural beauty that we had pictured it to be. We were now at a cross roads and hanging on to sanity by a thread. We made a decision to continue to drive through Australia. The children needed an education. The only way to give them an education was to teach them ourselves. One child would read the map in the front of the car while the other would sit in the back working through educational books we had brought along the way. We would stop off at parks so that our children could interact with other children of the same age! Times were getting harder and harder. Our life was in the back of our car and we didn't have a plan. We started to drive north of Brisbane back towards surfer's paradise and the Gold coast knowing that in reality it would be too expensive to settle there. But the beauty pulled us in. When we stopped off at a local park we could hear a family talking about a beautiful place not too far from Noosa that was cheap and up and coming. It was called Caloundra. It was also near a beautiful part of the world called Maroochydore. We looked at each other and made our plans to head that way. This place was pure paradise. The vibrant blue skies and a back drop of the glass House Mountains on one side and the beautiful ocean on the other. It was rich in wildlife and nestled in the rainforest. The sky was so clear that you could see the stars every night. They seemed to be so near that you could touch them. We would often pop down to the beach and feed the porpoises of the end of the pear at the end of the day. The place was full with organic shops and trust boxes. There were local cheese factories and honey factories and pineapple and macadamia nut farms. There was a mountain nearby called Melany. It stood proudly, showing off its splendour of natural lakes and local shops. This place was a living dream. It is where you could wander down the streets on a Sunday enjoying a coffee and basking in the sun. Whilst wandering you could pick up a little treasure from the craft stalls whilst a musician would play a lazy tune to set you in the mood. The children had now been to schools all across Australia and they seemed to be holding up fine. They were sociable and although my youngest child had her tantrums. All of the worries that she could be bipolar were fading into the distance or maybe that was what I had chosen to think. After enjoying two years of living a wonderful dream reality hit home when my husband had a phone call. His father had been poorly and he felt that it was time to go back and see him. I argued that he couldn't go on his own and that we should all fly back as a family just for a few months. Unfortunately my husband's father took a turn for the worst and needed a coronary by-pass. He lived another four months after this operation and then sadly passed away. My husband had worked with his father before we left for Australia. He now had to take on the responsibility of the business and support his mother financially. He took on his father's business to support the whole family. We became British residents once more. We had lived a dream that had enriched our lives but now we were back to reality where our feet hit firmly on the ground. Our youngest child started having problems at school and with the children in the street. She was bossy and argumentative but now there was another alarming signal. She could not deal with confrontation. I didn't notice all of the things that were happening around me. I guess you don't until it's too late. Life buzzes' by so quickly. For a whole year, she complained about feeling sick. She didn't want to attend school and yet every day I would tell her not to be silly and to get ready. I would walk her to the school gates and she would be kicking and screaming. I would have to drag her through the school gates. Her moods became increasingly erratic and aggressive and she had very low self esteem. She is however, a bright child and seemed eager to learn. One afternoon, just as I was about to leave home to collect my children from school I had a phone call from the school. The teacher on the phone was explaining to me about an incident that had taken place with my daughter and another child on a local trip out of school. The teacher had witnessed the incident and had said that it had made her blood go cold. She described the incident and that two children were involved. A child had forced a glass bottle of alcohol down my daughter's throat. She didn't know what was in the bottle. Was it alcohol, rain water or something worse, drugs or urine perhaps? I rushed up to the school to collect my child. As I reached the school it had became increasingly clear that the whole matter had been brushed under the carpet. The following day there was more to come and the other child in question punched my daughter in the stomach until she was winded. I know that these particular children were worried that the news would get out to their parents and that they would be severely reprimanded. They wanted to shut my daughter up. Things started to spiral out of control and our doubts of bi-polar were now arising again. Time after time we were called to the school for one problem after another. One exhausting day, enough was enough. Reality had hit and alarm bells started ringing. It was time to change schools. We viewed a local village school and moved our daughter within the week. The changes were almost instant, but there was still quite a bit of work to do to make her feel more confident. My daughter could not cope with confrontation. The school came up with an ingenious plan to use sign language if she needed time-out. This worked a treat. The old school rang me a few weeks later complaining of a letter that I hadn't signed for my youngest child entitling her to attend a trip. I just thanked them. The lady on the phone was curious to my reply. I just said thank you for helping make the right decision. My child left your school two weeks ago and you didn't even know. She is now at a new school and things are going well. I decided to do some research and I brought some books on explosive children and how to deal with a defiant child. As I started to read one particular book it dawned on me that this book could have been written about my daughter. My husband and I started reading all of the books that we could find. We started to work hard with our daughter trying to make things work out for her. We still do not know the outcome yet as she has not been assessed and probably never will be. What will an assessment do? Will it just label her or will it help her better her life. One thing is for sure. Bipolar must run in families. It must be passed down through our genes, just like red hair. How to live with it is hard. Strangers do not accept it. There seems to be relatively no help or guidance and mental health still seems to be a taboo. So far there has been no help for her. I would just like to understand what makes her mind tick the way it does. My husband says she is just wired differently from the rest of us. I know that my father's past had always been to both ends of extreme. He was almost wild at times and his anger and short temperedness has cost him so much. He could switch at a flick of a button. Sometimes he seemed to laugh as though he was going half mad before he would turn. Other times he would come across as very quiet before the switch would take place. You always had to be careful. You could never be sure of what would happen next. As an adult I find myself questioning my personality constantly. I sit here rattling off my deepest secrets. These are deep secrets that are about my childhood and how I terrified of my father and how I survived the extremes that were thrown at me and my family. As an adult I am still terrified of my former life. I seem to have a mix of personalities that makes me feel really insecure about myself. Maybe I too have a multiple personality disorder and although I do not agree that I was abused as a child, I still feel that my childhood has carved out the different personalities that I seem to have. I can no longer control my flood of emotions that still hit me in waves. On the bad days my body still shudders with past images and my mind works overtime with words echoing inside my soul. I feel that I seem to split into multiple selves. Over the years I have gone from being promiscuous at a very early age. Nothing was attached with feeling, this was a period of self abuse. I could be reckless, disappearing to London at the age of fourteen and not caring when I would return home. Sometimes I would not return for days at a time. School wasn't my safe haven and so I didn't really care if I missed it. Then there was the

Miss Perfect side and the hard working side. I was also very driven. I didn't worry about being stopped and this reckless side of me was mad and invincible. I believed that I could become anything. The sensitivity that I have is unbearable and I wish I could be colder hearted. I constantly worry about what others think of me. Still worrying long after I have had contact with that person. I would make up stories on how to make them like me again. I am still so vulnerable and delicate, just like a china cup that could be easily broken. All of these personalities would be masked by me pretending to be the life and soul of the party. I would always laugh the loudest and make the kindest comments. I would never really let my guard down and just be myself for a change. I could never relax or take time out for myself. Maybe now I am midway through my life I have started to integrate many of my personalities and I continue to try hard on becoming a better person for myself and my children. Note to myself: Life is exhausting and I will become powerful emotionally in a secure way. My childhood has most definitely been contradictory and complex just like me. I am still facing insecurity. Looking back now I see that I blocked the reality of the extreme and painful situations by not crying. I learnt to numb myself to all feelings and tears. Seeing the child psychiatrist taught me that I could only count on myself and only I could be brave enough to fix things. Although I find that sometimes the truth is too hard to take. My father is still battling with his temper. He has recently been awaiting a conviction for grievous bodily harm yet again. My daughters are my world and I will be there to help them in any way that I can. And me, well I smile as much as I can and I am eternally grateful that I have a loving family, great friends, my job and my dog who is my friend for life. I hope this book helps you understand many things and makes you understand how vulnerable we all are and that to read other people's emotions is a wonderful gift. Not all can explain our thoughts and feelings as we would like. Thank you for reading my story. xxx

## Did you know that Abuse is categorised as follows

### Emotional Abuse

Examples include but are not limited to: name-calling, belittling, yelling, screaming, threatening, not being emotionally available to a child, ignoring a child, extreme punishment for even minor infractions, isolation of child, etc.

### Physical Abuse

Examples include but are not limited to: hitting, kicking, punching, slapping, biting, shaking, pulling hair, bruising, cutting, burning, etc.

### Neglect

A pattern of failure to provide for a child's basic human needs including but not limited to: inadequate food, hygiene or shelter, disregard for a child's safety, leaving a child unattended, inadequate nurturing or affection, failure to ensure a child receives education, permitting a child to use alcohol or recreational drugs, delay or refusal to provide necessary medical care, etc

www.ingramcontent.com/pod-product-compliance
Lightning Source LLC
Chambersburg PA
CBHW020609300526
45785CB00021B/1528